James R. Hawley

The assassination and history of the conspiracy:

A complete digest of the whole affair from its inception to its culmination, sketches of the principal characters, reports of the obsequies, etc

James R. Hawley

The assassination and history of the conspiracy:
A complete digest of the whole affair from its inception to its culmination, sketches of the principal characters, reports of the obsequies, etc

ISBN/EAN: 9783337730499

Printed in Europe, USA, Canada, Australia, Japan

Cover: Foto ©ninafisch / pixelio.de

More available books at **www.hansebooks.com**

THE
ASSASSINATION

AND HISTORY OF

THE CONSPIRACY,

A complete digest of the whole affair from its inception to its culmination, Sketches of the principal Characters, Reports of the Obsequies, etc.

FULLY ILLUSTRATED.

CINCINNATI:
J. R. HAWLEY & Co., 164 Vine Street.
1865.

CONTENTS.

I.
Sketch of the Life of Abraham Lincoln.

II.
About Secret Organizations Connected with the Conspiracy, and their Influences.

III.
History of the Conspiracy—the Plot and Deeds.

IV.
The Assassins—their Pursuit and Capture.

V.
Sketches of the leading Conspirators.

VI.
Obsequies—the Funeral Cortege from City to City and final ceremonies at Springfield.

VII.
Incidents and Reminiscences.

ILLUSTRATIONS.

I. The Assassination of President Lincoln.

II. The Attempt on Secretary Seward.

III. Portrait of John Wilkes Booth.

IV. Capture and Death of Booth.

V. Portrait of Boston Corbett.

PREFACE.

The poignant grief and universal deeply seated sorrow of those who knew Abraham Lincoln best and loved him most—the native and adopted masses of our re-born republic—are not restricted to the millions who, by his wise policy and stern adherence to the right, may yet say to the down trodden of other lands. "Come as your brothers have come, our glorious Union is again intact, an asylum for the oppressed."

The dire calamity that has enshrouded our land with the ebony mantle of darkness is not ours alone. It is world wide. The mighty nations of Europe stand aghast at the dreadful deed.

Brittania's royal widow sympathizes with her

afflicted sister of Columbia. The Lion tames on beholding the agony of the bird of Jove. Gallia reverts to her Reign of Terror, and wonders whether rivers of blood will flow in America as in her days of Robespeirre. "Not so, Nephew of your Uncle." The mantle of Elijah has fallen upon Elisha; Columbia has an abiding faith in her Johnson.

Classic Italia drops her chisel at the unfinished statue; the pencil refuses its office at the canvas. Our Hosmer and Powers cease for awhile, and mentally ask "who shall bring forth from the marble the semblance of the noblest work of God—a GOOD MAN?

Lands of Kosciusko and Kossuth! weep, as well you may, for the martyred statesman, but despair not. Wait a little longer and all will be well for the cause of freedom. Dire calamities to nations bring forth heroic vindicators of the right, as did the dark spirits of slavery, and treason accursed, call to the helm of State that man who lived to witness the eradication of both those blasting influences from the land which he has honored no less than her people now, and will for all time, honor his memory.

Thanks to her noble Emperor, Russia's Bear has ceased his growl over serfdom, and the immortal edict of our Lincoln unrivets the shackles of four millions of *men* now—hitherto *slaves*. Well may they chant their homely but joyous ditty. "Now has the Kingdom come, in the year of Jubilee." Terrible as has been the ordeal through which the nation has passed, there remains the proud boast that she faltered not in her firm determination to sustain her position as the Land of Freedom, the home of the oppressed. Nay, more, her grandeur and power are now far greater than when the rebellious crew developed their hell-born schemes for which they now stand accursed of God and man.

The rainbow of promise dissipates the cloud of doubt as to the perpetuity of the Republic and all will soon be well.

The mighty drama is about to close. Four acts, of a year each, have been witnessed by an agonized audience of wailing widows and orphans.

The curtain will soon fall on the fifth. Vindicated justice, retribution and expiation of the atrocious deeds of traitors upon the gallows will be the fitting denouement of that tragedy to which generations unborn will turn with mingled feelings of wonder and horror.

Historians of futurity will be at fault as to upon whom of the two actors shall fall the fullest execration of all men—the bloodstained Assassin of the tragedy, or the pusillanimous, unsexed buffoon of the farce just enacted.

Such as the above were our first thoughts. To speak or write calmly now is a heavy task. The pulpit andthe rostrum have called forth the talent of the nation, but the theme is too great. Our Clay, Webster and Everett are no more.

We close our brief preface with a few remarks suggested in our calmer moments.

Among the declarations of JOHN FELTON, who assassinated the Duke of Buckingham, circumstances gave prominence to this: "There is no alliance nearer to any one than his country."

Every assassin of public men, and every rebel against the laws of his country, has probably persuaded himself that he was actuated by noble motives, and therefore anxious to blazon his spurious patriotism on the historic page. Under our institutions, true patriotism recognizes "the country" in its faithful and trustworthy representative, and the good President of the United States always becomes the object of unbounded endearment to the American people, with small regard to ordinary political bias on the part of any. When a man has carried our loved country through its sorest trials and greatest afflictions, he should find his reward in the country's deepest love; and if a deeper love exists than that with which loyal men to-day cherish the memory of the martyr President, its manifestations are unknown.

ABRAHAM LINCOLN was justly called the good President. From the first, he dared to do right, even contrary to great prejudice on the part of superficial judges; and his acts, during the stormy term of his administration, have formed for him a prouder monument than his bereaved people can ever dedicate to his name. Blocks of granite and marble shafts are not needed to perpetuate the memory of the Christian statesman and martyred patriot in the hearts of freemen everywhere on God's footstool; and through the record of his acts shall he evermore declare to the world; "I still live."

"Charity for all, malice toward none," was a declaration of his heart. The principle had marked his life, give emphasis to his acts, and imbued all his politics. That such a man could have a personal enemy is incomprehensible, and seems totally absurd, until explained as an offshoot of the secession malady that crazed the brains of his murderers, and fitted them, through its inquisitorial tuition, for the blackest crime; and, however matters may be patched, explained, apologized for or generally befogged, the common sense of the people will force them to view this damning act *only* as the grand culmination of the teachings of secession.

The horrible fact of the assassination of President LINCOLN needs slight comment here. The people have weighed it deliberately, and are calmly waiting for results that shall complete its expiation. They demand nothing unreasonable, and feel that the crime can be measured by no degree of punishment. Developments at this moment in progress are unraveling the dark intricacies of the most horrible conspiracy that ever stained our annals, and throughout the land the fervent petition for *justice* ascends to God from every loyal hamlet. Whatever the sacrifice, let justice be done.

The mighty pilot who guided our nation's bark through the perilous storm in safety, is cold in his grave, and the genius of liberty will ever mourn the irreparable loss. Let us profit by his great example, and strive to imitate his virtues.

ABRAHAM LINCOLN.

SKETCH OF HIS LIFE.

ABRAHAM LINCOLN was born in that part of Hardin county, Kentucky, which has since been called Larue. His remote ancestors were from Berks county, Pennsylvania. They removed to Rockingham county, Virginia, where Abraham the grandfather and Thomas the father of Mr. Lincoln were born. In 1780, Abraham Lincoln settled in Kentucky, which was at that time a wilderness filled with savages. His rude cabin was distant two or three miles from the nearest white settler. Life in this part of Kentucky was then in constant danger. The settler carried his gun and axe to the place of his daily labor, the one being as necessary to his protection as the other for the purposes of work. At night when the family retired to rest, the gun was always placed within convenient access.

For four years, Abraham Lincoln managed to escape, while whole families in the immediate vicinity were murdered by the Indians. At the end of that period, while engaged one day in clearing a piece of land about four miles from home, he was suddenly attacked and killed, and his scalped remains were found the next morning. The blow fell heavily on his widow, who was now alone in the wilderness with her three sons and two daughters, and very little money with which to procure the necessities of life. Compelled by poverty to separate, all the children but Thomas left the county, the second son removing to Indiana, the rest to other parts of Kentucky. Thomas at the age of twelve also left home, but soon returned to Kentucky, and in the year 1806 married Miss Nancy Hanks, who was a native of Virginia, so that all of the immediate ancestors of the President were born on Southern soil. Mrs. Lincoln could read but not write, while her husband could do neither, except to scribble his name in a style which only some of his most intimate friends could decipher. Regretting his own want of culture, he fully appreciated the advantages of education, and honored the superior learning of others. He was noted for kindness of heart and great industry and perseverance. Mrs. Lincoln, although possessed of no education, was blessed with much natural talent, excellent judgment and good sense. These qualifications, together with her great piety, made her a suitable partner for a man of Thomas Lincoln's attributes. She was a mother whose example and teaching could not fail to be of vast benefit in the formation of the characters of her children. This estimable couple had three children—a daughter, a son who died in infancy, and Abraham who was born on the 12th of February, 1809. The sister attained the years of womanhood and married, but died without issue.

Although Southern by birth and residence, Mr. Lincoln early became imbued with a disgust for slavery. In witnessing the evils of the "peculiar institution," he longed for freedom from the disagreeable effects of a condition of society which made a poor white man even more degraded than the negro. Entertaining these sentiments he naturally desired to change his place of residence. Early in October, 1816, finding a purchaser for his farm, he made arrangements for the transfer of the property and for his removal. Ten barrels of whisky of forty gallons each formed the consideration for the sale of the farm, and although Mr. Lincoln was a temperate man, he acceded to the terms, because such transactions were common and regarded as proper. The value of the whisky was two hundred and eighty dollars and twenty cents in money.

Mr. Lincoln, with the slight assistance little Abe could give him, prepared a flat-boat and was soon floating down the Rolling Fork river with his household goods, tools and the barrels of whisky on his way to Indiana. After he had left the Rolling Fork and reached the Ohio, his boat was upset and all on it thrown into the river. With the assistance of some men on the bank, he saved the boat and a few tools, axes and three barrels of whisky. Starting once more, and proceeding to a well known ferry on the river, he was guided into the interior by a resident of the section of country in which he had landed, to whom he gave his boat in payment for his services. He traveled for several days with much difficulty, most of the time being employed in cutting a road through the forest wide enough for a team, and at the end of eighteen miles, Spencer county, Indiana, was reached. The site of the new home being determined upon Mr. Lincoln returned to Kentucky on foot, and made preparations to remove his family. In a few days the party bade farewell to their old home, Mrs. Lincoln and her daughter riding one horse, the father another and Abe a third. After seven days' journey through an uninhabited country, their resting place at night being a blanket, spread upon the ground, they arrived at the spot selected for their residence, and no unnecessary delays were permitted to interfere with the immediate and successful clearing of a site for a cabin. An axe was placed in Abe's hands, and, with a neighbor's assistance, in two days Mr. Lincoln had a house of about eighteen feet square. It had only one room, but some slabs laid across logs overhead gave additional accommodations, which were reached by climbing a rough ladder in one corner. A bed, a table and four stools were then made by the two settlers, father and son, and the building was ready for occupancy. The loft was Abe's bed room, and there, night after night for many years, he who but recently occupied the most exalted position in the gift of the American people, and who dwelt in the White House at Washington, surrounded by all the comforts that wealth and power could give, slumbered with a coarse blanket for his mattress and another for his covering. Abe did not, through the long winter, neglect his reading and spelling. Before leaving Kentucky he had attended school, though for a short time only. He also practiced with the rifle, and became a shot of some note, much to the delight of his parents.

About a year after the family removed to Indiana, Mrs. Lincoln died. Abe felt the loss keenly. He had been a dutiful son, and she the most devoted of mothers. A young man, soon after Mrs. Lincoln's death, offered to teach Abe writing. The opportunity was fraught with too much benefit to be rejected, and after a few weeks practice, under eye of his instructor and also out of doors with a piece of chalk or charred stick, he was able to write his name, and in less than twelve months could write a letter.

Mr. Lincoln married during the next year, Mrs. Sally Johnston of Elizabethtown, Kentucky, a widow lady with three children. Between this lady and Abe a strong attachment sprung up. She was every way calculated to supply the place made vacant by the death of Mrs. Lincoln. At the time of Mr. Lincoln's second marriage, a person named Crawford moved into the neighborhood and opened a school to which Abe was sent. At this school he improved very much in reading and writing, and mastered arithmetic. "His school-garb comprised a suit of dressed buckskin and a cap made from a raccoon skin." He took an unusual pride in his studies, and close application and a retentive memory made him a favorite scholar with this teacher. He was employed by the most ignorant settlers as their scribe whenever they had letters to write. A brief period at this school, and, to use a common phrase, his education was finished. Six months of instruction within the walls of an insignificant schoolhouse is all the education that Abraham Lincoln has received during a long lifetime.

For four or five years after leaving school, or until he was eighteen, he constantly labored in the woods with his axe, cutting down trees and splitting rails, and during the evening, read such works as he could obtain among the settlers. A year after, he was hired, by a man living near, at ten dollars a month, to go to New Orleans on a flat-boat, loaded with stores, which were destined for sale at the plantations on the Mississippi river, near the Crescent city, and with but one companion, started on this rather dangerous journey. At night they tied up alongside of the bank and rested upon the hard deck, with a blanket for a covering, and during the hours of light whether their lonely trip was cheered by a bright sun, or made disagreeable in the extremely violent storms, their craft floated down the stream, its helmsmen never for a moment losing their spirits, or regretting their acceptance of the positions they occupied. Nothing occurred to mar the success of the trip, nor the excitement naturally incident to a flat-boat expedition of some eighteen hundred miles, save a midnight attack by a party of negroes, who, after a severe conflict, were whipped by Abe and his comrade, and compelled to flee. After selling their goods at a handsome profit, the young merchants returned to Indiana.

Mr. Lincoln removed to Illinois in 1830, carrying their household articles thither in large wagons drawn by oxen, Abe being the driver of one team. In two weeks they reached Decatur, Macon County, Illinois, near the center of the State, and in another day, were on a tract of land of ten acres, on the north side of the Sangamon river, about ten miles west of Decatur. Immediately after their arrival, a log cabin was erected, and Abe commenced to split the rails for the fence, with which the place was to be enclosed. As a rail splitter, a tiller of the soil, or a huntsman, to whose great accuracy of aim the family depended in a great measure, for their daily food, young Abraham Lincoln was active, earnest and laborious, and when in the following spring, he made known his intention to leave his home, to seek his fortune among strangers, the tidings were received by his parents and friends with the most profound sorrow. Packing up his clothing, he started westward, and engaged to work on a farm in Menard county. Here he remained during the summer and winter, at the same time improving himself in reading, writing, grammar and arithmetic. Early in the following spring he was hired by a man named Offutt, to assist in taking a flatboat to New Orleans, and as it was found impossible to purchase a suitable boat, Abe lent a willing and industrious hand in building one at Sagamon, from whence, when completed, it was floated into the Mississippi river. The trip was made, and his employer was so much gratified with the industry and tact of his hired hand, that he engaged him to take charge of his mill and store in the village of New Salem. In this position, Honest

Abe as he was now called, won the respect and confidence of all with whom he had business dealings, while socially, he was much beloved by the residents, young and old, of the place.

The Black Hawk war broke out in the early part of the following year, and the governor of Illinois calling for troops, Abe offered his services. He placed his name first on the roll at the recruiting station in New Salem, and by his influence induced many of his friends and companions to do likewise. A company was soon formed, and Abe was unanimously elected captain. The company marched to Bardstown, and from there to the seat of war; but during their term of enlistment—thirty days—were not called into active service. A new levy was then called for and he enlisted as a private, and at the end of thirty days reenlisted, and remained with his regiment until the end of the war.

Soon after his return from this campaign, he was waited upon by several of the influential citizens of New Salem, who asked him his consent to nominate him for the Legislature. He had been a resident of the county only nine months but as a thorough-going "Henry Clay man" was needed, he was deemed the most suitable person to run. There were eight aspirants for the legistive position, but although he received *two hundred and seventy-seven* votes out of *two hundred and eighty-four* cast in New Salem he was not elected, the successful candidate leading by a few votes, having received a heavy vote in the country.

He engaged in the mercantile business soon after his defeat, but in a few months sold out, and under the tuition of John Calhoun—in later years connected with the Lecompton Convention—became proficient in surveying, an occupation which for more than a year he found very remunerative for a novice. He was for a time post-master at New Salem.

In August, 1834, he was elected to the Legislature, and in 1836, 1838 and 1840 was re-elected. He determined to become a lawyer while attending the first session of the Legislature to which he was elected, and being placed in possession of the necessary books, through the kindness of Hon. John T. Stuart, applied himself to study, and in 1836 was admitted to practice at the bar. He became a partner of Mr. Stuart at Springfield in 1837.

In March, 1837, a protest was presented to the House of Representatives of Illinois, and signed by Daniel Stone and Abraham Lincoln, Representatives from Sangamon county. This is the first record that we have of the sentiments of Mr. Lincoln on the slavery question. It was in opposition to a series of resolutions which had been adopted, taking an extreme Southern view of slavery, for which Mr. Lincoln refused to vote, and subsequently handed in the protest.

Mr. Lincoln was a Whig candidate for Presidential elector in every campaign from 1836 to 1852, and in 1844 he stumped the entire State of Illinois for Henry Clay, and going into Indiana spoke daily to large gatherings, until the day of the election. His style of speaking was pleasing to the masses of the people, and his earnest appeals were not only well received, but were productive of much benefit to his favorite candidate. He was accustomed, from early childhood, to the habits and peculiarities of all kinds of people, and he knew exactly what particular style of language best suited his hearers, and the result was that he was always listened to with a degree of attention and interest which few political speakers received.

Mr. Lincoln was elected to Congress from the central district of Illinois in 1846, by a majority of over 1500 votes—the largest ever given in that district for a candidate opposed to the Democratic party. Illinois elected seven representatives that year and all were Democrats but Mr. Lincoln. In the Whig convention of 1848, he was an active delegate, and earnestly advocated the selection of General Taylor as the nominee for the Presidency.

He was a candidate before the Legislature of Illinois for U. S. Senator, but his political opponents were in the majority, and General Shields was chosen. From that time till 1854, he confined himself to his profession. In the latter year he again entered the political field and battled indefatigably in the celebrated campaign which resulted in victory for the first time to the opposition of the Democratic party in Illinois. During the canvass Mr. Lincoln was frequently brought into controversy upon the stand with Stephen A. Douglas. One of the discussions that was held on the fourth of October, 1854, during the progress of the Annual State Fair, being remarkable as the great discussion of the campaign.

On the second of June, 1858, the Republican State Convention met at Springfield, and nominated Mr. Lincoln as their candidate for the United States Senate. The contest which followed was one of the most exciting and remarkable ever witnessed in this country. Mr. Douglas his opponent, had few superiors as a political debater, and while he had made many enemies, by his course upon the Nebraska bill, his personal popularity had been greatly increased by his independence, and by the opposition manifested to him by the Administration.

During the campaign Mr. Lincoln spoke thus of the Declaration of Independence:

"These communities, (the thirteen colonies,) by their representatives in old Independence Hall, said to the world of men, 'We hold these truths to be self-evident that all men are born equal; that they are endowed by their Creator with inalienable rights; that among these are life, liberty and the pursuit of happiness.' This was their majestic interpretation of the economy of the universe. This was their lofty, wise and noble understanding of the justice of the Creator to His creatures. Yes, gentlemen, to all His creatures, to the whole great family of man. In their enlightened belief, nothing stamped with the Divine image and likeness, was sent into the world to be trodden on and degraded and imbruted by its fellows. They grasped not only the race of men then living, but they reached forward and seized upon the furthest posterity. They created a beacon to guide their children, and their children's children, and the countless myriads who should inhabit the earth in other ages. Wise statesmen as they were, they knew the tendency of prosperity to breed tyrants, and so they established these great self-evident truths that when in the distant future some man, some faction, some interest, should set up the doctrine that none but rich men, or none but white men, or none but Anglo-Saxon white men, were entitled to life, liberty and the pursuit of happiness their posterity might look up again to the Declaration of Independence, and take courage to renew the battle which their fathers began, so that truth and justice and mercy, and all the humane and christian virtues, might not be extinguished from the land, so that no man would, hereafter, dare to limit and circumscribe the great principles on which the temple of liberty was being built.

"Now, my countrymen, if you have been taught doctrines conflicting with the great landmarks of the Declaration of Independence, if you have listened to suggestions which would take away from its grandeur, and mutilate the fair symmetry of its proportions, if you have been inclined to believe that all men are not created equal in those inalienable rights enumerated by our chart of liberty, let me entreat you to come back, return to the fountain whose waters spring close by the blood of the Revolution. Think nothing of me, take no thought for the political fate of any man whomsoever, but come back to the truths that are in the Declaration of Independence.

"You may do any thing with me you choose, if you will but heed these sacred principles. You may not only defeat me for the Senate, but you may take me and put me to death. While pretending no indifference to earthly honors, I *do claim* to be actuated in this contest by something higher than an anxiety for office. I charge you to drop every paltry and insignificant thought for any man's success. It is nothing, I am nothing, Judge Douglas is nothing. *But do not destroy that immortal emblem of humanity, the Declaration of American Independence.*"

The election day at length arrived, and although the efforts of Mr. Lincoln resulted in an immense increase of Republican votes, whatever aspirations he had for personal success were frustrated. A vote of 126,084 was cast for the Republican candidates, 121,940 for the Douglas Democrats and 5,091 for the Lecompton candidates, but Mr. Douglas was elected United States Senator by the Legislature, in which his supporters had a majority of eight on joint ballot.

On the sixteenth of May, 1860, the Republican National Convention assembled in Chicago, for the purpose of nominating candidates for the Presidency and Vice-Presidency. On the third ballot Mr. Lincoln came within one of being nominated.

One of the delegates then changed four votes of his State, giving them to Mr. Lincoln, thus nominating him.

On the sixth of November, 1860, the election for President took place with the following result. Mr. Lincoln received 491,275 votes over Mr. Douglas; 1,018,499 over Mr. Breckinridge and 1,275,821 over Mr. Bell; and the vote was subsequently proclaimed by Congress as follows:

> For Abraham Lincoln, of Illinois...180
> For John C. Breckinridge, of Kentucky................................. 72
> For John Bell, of Tennessee... 39
> For Stephen A. Douglas, of Illinois.. 12

INCEPTION OF THE PLOT.

A leading officer of the Buchanan Administration received, on the first of January, 1861, a letter from a friend, a gentleman of Southern sympathies living in Baltimore, in which among other things, it was stated that twelve thousand men were already enrolled and organized in that city, bound by the most solemn oaths, to do the bidding of their leaders, whose purpose was to march them against Washington, capture it, and with such reinforcements as they could get from the south, hold it, not only to prevent the inauguration of Mr. Lincoln, but in order to make it the capital of the future Southern Republic. Still darker threats than this, the letter stated, were whispered about, being nothing less than the assassination of Mr. Lincoln and Mr. Hamlin. At that time, it is well known, bets were freely made in the streets of Washington that Mr. Lincoln would never be inaugurated as President of the United States. These stories were shortly after denied, but subsequent events prove that they have some foundation.

On the 11th of February, Mr. Lincoln left his home in Springfield, Illinois, on his way to Washington. A large number of people assembled, to pay him a token of respect before his departure. The moment was a solemn one. The reports of threatened assassination, forcible prevention of the inauguration, and the like, had reached his ears, as well as those of his townsmen. His speech was short but affecting. He said:

"My friends: No one in my position can appreciate the sadness I feel at this parting. To this people I owe all that I am. Here I have lived more than a quarter of a century; here my children were born, and here one of them lies buried. I know not how I shall see you again. A duty devolves upon me which is greater, perhaps, than that which devolved upon any other man since the days of Washington. He never would have succeeded except for the aid of Divine Providence, upon which he at all times relied. I feel that I cannot succeed without the same Divine aid which sustained him, and on the same Almighty Being I place my reliance for support; and I hope you, my friends, will all pray that I may receive that Divine assistance without which I cannot succeed, but with which success is certain. Again I bid you all an affectionate farewell."

During this speech Mr. Lincoln betrayed much emotion, and hundreds in the crowd were affected to tears; cries of "We will pray for you," "be just and have no fear" were heard, and a feeling of deep solemnity settled over the whole assemblage.

Leaving Springfield Mr. Lincoln proceeded by easy passages to Indianapolis, Cincinnati, Columbus, Pittsburgh, Cleveland, Buffalo, Albany and New York. At all these places he was warmly received. Having been welcomed to the city in the presence of the Common Council of New York, by Mayor Wood, he replied:

"Mr. Mayor:—It is with feelings of deep gratitude that I make my acknowledgment for the reception which is given me in the great commercial city of New York. I cannot but remember that this is done by people who do not by a majority agree with me in political sentiment. It is more grateful because in this I see that for the great principles of our Government the people are nearly all or quite unanimous. In regard to the diffi-

THE ATTEMPTED ASSASSINATION OF SECRETARY SEWARD.

culties that confront us at this time, and of which your Honor has thought fit to speak so becomingly and so justly, as I suppose, I can only say that I agree in the sentiments expressed by the Mayor.

"In my devotion I hope I am behind no man in the Union. But as for the wisdom with which to conduct the affairs tending to the preservation of the Union, I fear that too great confidence may have been reposed in me. I am sure I bring a devoted heart to the work. There is nothing that could ever bring me to consent, willingly, to the destruction of this Union, under which, not only the great commercial city of New York but the whole country has acquired its greatness, unless it were to be for that thing for which the Union itself was made. I understand the ship to be made for the carrying of the cargo, and so long as the ship can be sailed with the cargo it should never be abandoned. This Union should never be abandoned unless it fails, and the possibility of its preservation shall cease to exist, without throwing passengers and cargo overboard. So long, then, as it is possible that the prosperity and liberties of this people can be preserved in the Union it shall be my purpose at all times to preserve it. And now, Mr. Mayor, again thanking you for the reception which has been given me, allow me to draw to a close."

During this day (February 20th) reports of the threatened assassination of the President were circulated in the streets. At Newark, N. J., a handbill was circulated, calling upon unemployed working-men to attend at the depot on Mr. Lincoln's arrival at that city, and "demonstrate their differences" with him.

A meeting was held in the evening, and a large number

of persons volunteered for a cavalry escort. At Trenton a large additional police force was put on duty to preserve order. No disturbance took place however. Mr. Lincoln arrived at Philadelphia on the evening of the 21st, and was enthusiastically received, as he had been at Newark, Rahway, New Brunswick, Princeton, Trenton, and other points along the route. Leaving Philadelphia on the morning of the 22d, he reached Harrisburgh in the happiest manner by the authorities and people of the city. Here, for the first time, rumors began to avail of persons being colluded together for some evil purpose.

The committee of arrangements at Harrisburg learning on creditable authority, that in all probability an attempt would be made on the President's life at Baltimore, debated the question of the manner of his passage—whether he should pass from depot to depot, or go by a route which avoided change of cars. Finally it was arranged to leave Harrisburgh at 6 o'clock in the evening, arriving at Baltimore and Washington at hours different from those heretofore announced. Accordingly Mr. Lincoln left Harrisburgh at the time secretly determined upon. The plan of action which was successfully carried out was this. Speeches and receptions were to be kept up all the afternoon; special trains were arranged, the telegraph silenced, and men were stationed to cut the wires if necessary; and upon the arrival in Baltimore, Mr. Lincoln was to be conveyed through the city in a close carriage. The plan was laid before Mr. Lincoln, and it is said he indignantly rejected it. Mrs. Lincoln begged of him to go, and Governor Curtin and other influential men also entreated him to adopt the plan. He was assured that he would certainly be assassinated if he followed the original programme; and it is said that Mrs. Lincoln's tears, and the arguments of his friends finally persuaded him to adopt the proposed course. He proceeded to Baltimore by a special express train, passed through the city unobserved, and reached Washington at 6 o'clock on the morning of the 24th. The train containing Mrs. Lincoln and the rest of the Presidental party left Harrisburgh at the time publicly announced. When it reached Baltimore a vast crowd had assembled to meet it; but it had got abroad that Mr. Lincoln had already passed through the city, and the train was saluted with groans and hisses. No violence was offered, however.

It is well here to state, in justice to the character of our murdered President, that the story published in the telegraphic dispatches of the New York Times, on the 24th of February, that Mr. Lincoln passed from Harrisburgh to Washington attired in a "Scotch plaid cap and very long military cloak, so that he was entirely unrecognizable," was utterly false. It was made out of whole cloth by a sensation reporter whose recent familiarity with Presidential attributes is fresh in the minds of the public. Mr. Lincoln was very much opposed to any concealment, but his opinion was overborne by that of undoubted personal and political friends. When he did go, however, he made no change in his costume, and no attempt at concealment.

The features of the Baltimore plot have never been perfectly made clear. Innumerable rumors prevailed at the time, some of them doubtless founded on fact, others simply absurd. On the evening of the 21st of February, 1861, Secretary (then

Senator) Seward received official intelligence from General Scott, that a most diabolical plot had been successfully arranged on the part of a secret organization in Baltimore to assassinate the President-elect on his arrival at that city. Mr. Seward communicated this intelligence to a few private friends, and it was determined to despatch a message at once to Philadelphia to inform Mr. Lincoln of the fact. On being told of it, the intended victim replied that he had heard the same thing from other sources, giving the Baltimore chief of police as one authority. The plot was to throw the Presidential train off the track by a torpedo placed conveniently to some high embankment, or failing in this, to mob and assassinate Mr. Lincoln on his arrival in Baltimore, the conspirators to surround the depot, armed with knife or pistol. Ten or fifteen men were said to have been prepared to complete the work, and it is reported that a vessel was lying in the harbor ready to convey the murderers to Mobile. The following account is taken from a source every way worthy of credit.

"Some of Mr. Lincoln's friends having heard that a conspiracy existed to assassinate him on his way to Washington, set on foot an investigation of the matter. For this purpose they employed a detective of great experience, who was engaged at Baltimore in the business some three weeks prior to Mr. Lincoln's expected arrival there, employing both men and women to assist him. Shortly after coming to Baltimore the detective discovered a combination of men banded together under a solemn oath to assassinate the President-elect. The leader of the conspiracy was an Italian refugee, a barber, well-known in Baltimore, who assumed the name of Orsini as indicative of the part he was to perform. The assistants employed by the detective, who, like himself, were strangers in Baltimore city, by assuming to be Secessionists from Louisiana and other seceding States, gained the confidence of some of the conspirators, and were intrusted with their plans. It was arranged in case Mr. Lincoln should pass safely over the railroad to Baltimore, that the conspirators should mingle with the crowd which might surround his carriage, and by pretending to be his friends, be enabled to approach his person, when, upon a signal from their leader, some of them would shoot at Mr. Lincoln with their pistols, and would throw into his carriage handgrenades filled with detonating powder, similar to those used in the attempted assassination of the Emperor Louis Napoleon. It was intended that in the confusion which should result from this attack, the assailants would escape to a vessel, which was waiting in the harbor to receive them, and be carried to Mobile, in the seceding State of Alabama.

"Upon Mr. Lincoln's arrival in Philadelphia, upon Thursday, the 21st day of February, a detective visited Philadelphia, and submitted to certain friends of the President-elect the information he had collected as to the conspirators and their plans. An interview was immediately arranged between Mr. Lincoln and the detective. The interview took place in Mr. Lincoln's room, in the Continental Hotel, where he was staying during his visit to Philadelphia.

"Mr. Lincoln, having heard the officer's statement, informed him that he had promised to raise the American flag on Independence Hall the next morning—the morning of the anniversary of Washington's Birthday—and that he had accepted the invitation of the Pennsylvania Legislature to be publicly received by that body in the afternoon of the same day. 'Both of these engagements,' said he, with emphasis, 'I will keep, if it costs me my life. If, however, after I have concluded these engagements, you can take me in safety to Washington, I will place myself at your disposal, and authorize you to make such arrangements as you may deem proper for that purpose.'

"On the next day in the morning Mr. Lincoln performed the ceremony of raising the American flag on Independence Hall in Philadelphia according to his promise, and arrived at Harrisburg on the afternoon of the same day, when he was formally welcomed by the Pennsylvania Legislature. After the reception he retired to his hotel, the Jones' House, and withdrew with a few confidential friends to a private apartment. Here he remained until nearly six o'clock the next morning, when in company with Colonel Lamon, he quietly entered a carriage without observation, and was driven to the Pennsylvania Railroad, where a special train for Philadelphia was waiting for him. Simultaneously with his departure from Harrisburg the telegraph wires were cut, so that his departure, if it should become known, might not be communicated at a distance.

"The special train arrived in Philadelphia at a quarter before 11 o'clock at night. Here he was met by the detective who had a carriage in readiness into which the party entered, and were driven to the depot of the Philadelphia Wilmington, and Baltimore Railroad.

"They did not reach the depot until a quarter past 11; but fortunately for them, the regular train, the hour of which for starting was 11, had been delayed. The party then took berths in the sleeping-car, and without change of cars passed directly through to Washington, where they arrived at the usual hour, $6\frac{1}{2}$ o'clock on the morning of Saturday, the 23d. Mr. Lincoln wore no disguise whatever, but journeyed in an ordinary traveling-dress.

"It is proper to state here that prior to Mr. Lincoln's arrival in Philadelphia, General Scott and Senator Seward in Washington had been apprised from independent sources that imminent danger threatened Mr. Lincoln in case he should publicly pass through Baltimore, and accordingly a special messenger, Mr. Frederick W. Seward, was dispatched to Philadelphia to urge Mr. Lincoln to come direct to Washington in a quiet manner. The messenger arrived in Philadelphia late on Thursday night, and had an interview with the President-elect immediately subsequent to his interview with the detective. He was informed that Mr. Lincoln would arrive by the early train on Saturday morning, and, in accordance with this information, Mr. Washburne, member of Congress from Illinois, awaited the President-elect at the depot in Washington, whence he was taken in his carriage to his quarters in Willard's Hotel, where Secretary Seward stood ready to receive him.

"The detective traveled with Mr. Lincoln under the name of E. J. Allen, which name was registered with the President-elect in the book at Willard's Hotel. Being a well-known individual, he was speedily recognized, and suspicion naturally arose that he had been instrumental in exposing the plot which caused Mr. Lincoln's hurried journey. It was deemed prudent that he should leave Washington two days after his arrival, although he had intended to remain and witness the ceremonies of inaugeration.

"After the discovery of the plot, a strict watch was kept by the agents of detection over the movements of the conspirators, and efficient measures were adopted to guard against any attack which they might meditate upon the President-elect until he was installed in office.

"Mr. Lincoln's family left Harrisburgh for Baltimore, on their way to Washington, in the special train intended for him; and, as before starting, a message announcing Mr. Lincoln's departure and arrival at Washington had been telegraphed to Baltimore over wires which had been repaired that morning, the passage through Baltimore was safely effected.

"The remark of Mr. Lincoln during the ceremony of raising the flag on Independence Hall on Friday morning, that he would assert his principles on his inaugeration, although he were to be assassinated on the spot, had evident reference to the communication made to him by the detective on the night preceding.

"The number originally ascertained to be banded together for the assassination of Mr. Lincoln was twenty, but the number of those who were fully apprised of the details of the plot became daily smaller as the time for executing it drew near.

"Some of the women employed by the detective went to serve as waiters, seamstresses, etc., in the families of the conspirators, and a record was regularly kept of what was said and done to further their enterprise. A record was also kept by the detective of their deliberations in secret conclave. The detective and his agents regularly contributed money to pay the expenses of the conspiracy."

Threats were made after Mr. Lincoln's first inaugeration. It is well known, that he reached Washington in safety, but the secession element vastly predominated at the Capital, and threats of violence to the President-elect and to Mr. Hamlin, and of the forcible suspension of the inaugeration, were neither few nor secret. The city was filled with rebels who proclaimed their sentiments boldly in the streets, and hinted violence to the Executive. National airs were hissed down in public places of amusement, loyal men were assaulted on the avenue, and cheers for Jeff. Davis were of common occurrence.

For some time previous to the inaugeration there had been threats of bloodshed on that occasion and the military authorities taxed their brains for devices to prevent any such catastrophe. Geneaal Scott made every preparation for fighting. The volunteer organizations in the procession were supplied with cartridges; sharpshooters were posted at convenient spots along the avenue and on the roofs of buildings, and at the market house a small force of infantry was posted for the support of the riflemen in that vicinity.

The batteries of Magruder and Fry were at the corner of Delaware Avenue and B street, ready for action; the gunners and drivers remaining at ther posts throughout the ceremonies. General Scott in the meantime kept his scouts busily occupied visiting all parts of the dense crowd, and watching for the first indications of trouble. The day passed off however quietly. But the feverish anxiety of that morning, and the certainty of terrible bloodshed following any riotous demonstrations, created impressions on the minds of those who were present, that will probably never be erased. The commandant Magruder of one of those batteries referred to, left Washington a few days after and subsequently was made a general by the rebels. Despite all the plans to the contrary the inauguration happily passed off without the occurrence of any scenes of violence of a similar character, the fighting being confined to drunken partisans in the street.

Since 1861, Mr. Lincoln has rarely, if ever, appeared in public without a sufficient escort, one company of cavalry being inevitable in attendance. Of late, however, it has been thought that precaution was not so absolutely necessary, and in the visit to the theatre at which it was destined he should be murdered, he was accompanied by no person save members of his own family and one officer of the army. However, great danger is known to be, after a time we became indifferent to it and neglect precautions that were at first deemed necessary. Not only was it all important that there should be a guard in constant attendance on the President, but so long as there was the least reason for suspicion of plots to destroy him, every effort ought to have been made to ferret out the schemers and bring them to justice, that an example be made. Had desperadoes been made to feel that so sure as they were discovered in any such undertakings, punishment the most severe was to follow, few would design a conspiracy and none possibly attempt to execute.

The last inauguration, however, did not pass off without a due proportion of rumors; and, amongst these was one that something was going on, indicating that trouble was anticipated from some undeveloped quarter. Rumor had it that all the roads leading to Washington had been heavily picketed for some days, and the bridges guarded with extra vigilance, as if on the watch for suspicious characters. Also, that the Eighth Illinois Cavalry had been pushed out from Fairfax Court House, on an active scouting expedition, as if in search of some of the same suspicious characters; and further, that undue proportion of hard cases, in grizzled costume, were to be seen upon the streets, indicating something pertending. But as the day wore on in tranquillity, all fears were dissipated. For the purpose of preserving order, the military patrols were doubled, and made more frequent rounds of the streets than usual. But notwithstanding the large number of strangers in the city, good order prevailed and but few arrests were made by the military or police authorities.

On the 7th of March, in the present year, a man named Clemens was arrested in Washington, chargee with having contemplated the assassination of the President. The facts in the case are as follows:—Clemens and another person came from Alexandria on inaugeration day. They were both extremely disorderly, and seemed to have been drinking freely. Clemens, in particular, was very abusive. He said, using gross and profane language, that he came to Washington to kill the President; that he was late by about one-half hour, and that his Saviour would never forgive him for failing to do so; that he would do it that night, namely, the 4th day of March; and that he came expressly to do it, and he would do it before he left town. He furthermore said that the Government has robbed him of a certain sum of money. This was the substance of an affidavit. Clemens was turned over from the military to the civil authorities, and was committed to jail for trial by the Court. Afterward he was released, as having been completely under the influence of liquor at the time the alleged threats were made, that he did not know what he said. But would it be remarkable, in view of present circumstances, if this man Clemens should really have had, or have, some connection with the real assassin of the President in carrying out the dreadful plot. It will be seen from Washington despatches that letters found in the trunk of Booth, the murderer, show that the assassination was originally fixed for the 4th of March, but postponed for some reason not yet known. Clemens declared that he also intended to murder Mr. Lincoln on that day.

SECRET ORGANIZATIONS.

Secret societies are of two kinds, those whose proceedings are unknown to all who do not belong to them; and those whose existence as well as transactions is kept inviolate. Of the second kind are those which have their origin and being in Europe, mostly in Italy, where they ought to remain. The American soil is no place for them. Societies of this kind are destructive of liberty, and the only means of suppressing them when they are found to exist is to bring to bear such an opposition of public opinion, that respectable persons will have nothing to do with them. No good in a land of freedom will come from organizations of this nature. What a man is unwilling to acknowledge openly, in reference to his political leanings and convictions, will generally be found to be in antagonism to the principles on which the government is based. Free discussion of all questions relating to the public weal is not only to be encouraged, but should be deemed absolutely necessary. We can never expect to advance in political science so long as the votes of enough to decide contests can be bought or controled by a few. If a number of persons in secret conclave, oath bound, are allowed to sway the masses, that they may ride into power and retain it, popular government is but a name, a sound, and an aristocracy becomes in effect the government.

The liberties of a people are not lost at once. The gradation is not rapid even. Slowly in most cases, but not the less surely the process goes on, and not till some violent measure is adopted by those who are thus seeking to deprive the people of their rights, do they wake up to a sense of their situation. And then it is found that what was once nothing more than a simple assertion of right has become treason against a person, or set of persons, who were originally nothing more than the agents of the people.

Extreme measures always beget extremes. Violence will be followed by violence, and there is no better way to bring about a despotism than by the commission of such deeds as those of the 14th of April. Stringent means will be adopted in such cases to capture the guilty ones, and many persons who are really innocent of all complicity in the affair will be suspected, and perhaps punished. The attention of every law-abiding citizen and well-wisher of his country must be drawn to the investigation going on. All are alike interested, and he who appears indifferent is morally an abettor. Sneers at those who assert that secret bodies exist must not be heeded. There do exist treasonable combinations whose purpose is, first, destruction of those in power, and finally subversion of republican institutions.

PLOTTING ORGANIZATIONS.

"There can be no reasonable doubt that Lincoln and Seward have been assassinated. The crimes of these two men may make this event justifiable in the eyes of man and God, but we do not concur with those who rejoice. Johnson has greater native ability, if this has not been impaired by his excesses, than any Northern statesman of his party except Chase. The war will now assume a new phase. If confined to these States, then it is one of utter extermination. The veritable Reign of Terror has already begun in Tennessee. *It is probable, if Booth be a Northern man, that the assassination of Lincoln is the work of those secret Western clubs whose mysteries have been developed in late judicial proceedings in Chicago and Ohio. If this be true, the war may begin in the North-west.*

"All the decency of the North was recently thoroughly disgusted by Johnson's conduct on the occasion of his inauguration as Vice-President. His drunken speech was illustrative of his character, and of the old adage, *in vino veritas.*

"He is a veritable 'plebeian,' a leveler, a *sans culotte.* However wedded to Johnson's theories of radicalism may have been the Republican newspapers, a few of them dared to mollify his violation of all laws of civilized decency. *Copperheadism could have inflicted upon the vanity and self-re-*

spect Puritanism no wound so deep as that which sent Lincoln to perdition and elevated Johnson to the throne. He hastened to assume the royal purple, and despite the recent military triumphs, the pride of the North was never so humiliated as at this very hour."—*Meridian (Miss.) Clarion.*

The italicised portions of the above extract point unmistakably to the Knights of the Golden Circle, or, as they are latterly known, Sons of Liberty; and convey information that is anything but guess-work on the part of the author. Matter coming to us in this semi-official form is abundant confirmation of all our preconceived suspicions, and we are fully assured that the damnable conspiracy that culminated in the murder of our beloved President, was incubated in the temples of this cursed league of the Circle, and that its minions in the persons of Booth, Harrold, Payne, Surratt, and their associates, were let loose upon their victims as the more active agents of this treasonable association. The rapid, positive and thoroughly systematic development of facts by the investigators of the assassination conspiracy is daily offering proof in support of this theory, if, indeed, it is not already demonstrated; and, if the proofs are really conclusive, what further outrage by this compact with hell are our people waiting for, before they arise in their might and destroy it? Has it not been treated as a myth long enough? And where its existence was known, have not its vagaries and mummery been sufficiently laughed at to allow people to give it a little serious attention just now? After this evidence of its power and outrageous designs, are there any weak enough to believe it impalpable, or simply the matter for pleasantry? Such are in danger; and our country is in imminent danger until the destructive elements germinated by this pestiferous order are searched out and thoroughly expurgated from our politics!

Knights Illini, and similar quackeries, are scarcely congenial to the spirit of Republican Institutions, and were never organized to perpetuate the government our fathers established through great tribulation. They are seeking strange gods, as outrè and distasteful to the public weal as the prostituted representative of Reason in the Reign of Terror. Ben. Allen, the Grand Seigneur of Copperheadism in New York, declared at the Democratic National Convention at Chicago, last year: "*The people will soon rise, and if they cannot put Lincoln out of power by the ballot, they will by the bullet.*" This declaration was received with loud cheers, and thereupon S. S. Cox, C. C. Burr, Koontz of Pennsylvania, Baker of Michigan, Stambaugh of Ohio, and several other delegates gave utterance to similar choice opinions,—each calling our President a usurper, and denouncing against him all the most outrageous crimes known to our laws. Threats of assassination were not made vaguely, but if the Copperhead chiefs meant what they publicly declared, every one of them should be indicted as accessories before the fact, and tried without ceremony.

The order of the Knights of the Golden Circle is not confined to the North-west, as rebel authority would have us believe, but is co-extensive with secession proclivities everywhere. It was an invention of the Secession movement years ago, when Jackson forced the poisonous hydra to secrete itself in dark and unfrequented places, and deposit its slime where it would not be contagious; but copperheadism could not thrive without it, and it was imported from the South to force the growth of a Northern party with Southern sympathies. It has existed in our midst during the past four years, but we hardly comprehend the fact; and still less do the people know of the nature and unholy purposes of the organization. It is time these particulars are fully understood. Its oaths and penalties, its spy system and police regulations, all its murderous ingenuity and damnable crimes, should be made public, that we may know the enemy we have to contend against; and that the people may know what a mine has been planted beneath their homes, in many cases by their own neighbors, to blow them to destruction in a moment. The "exposition" of EDMUND WRIGHT, first published about a year since, was scarcely heeded, although widely read. The Knights jeered at it, and called it incredible; but their object is now evident enough to thinking men, for of course they saw plainly that if WRIGHT was believed, their power was at an end. It is time now to heed every warning, and to break, permanently, the power of this oligarchy of devils. It is more dangerous to our liberties to-day than all the armies the South have had in the field have ever been; it works in secret, and we can have no notice of its intentions to sally forth to burn, pillage and murder. Its oaths are binding as words can make them; its penalties are terrible as the foulest devises of the Spanish Inquisition; its police regulations are on a large scale, carefully and systematically arranged; and all the guards that ingenuity can invent are thrown out to prevent recursancy. It is sworn to support the South, at any and all hazards, in every attempt to subvert our government; and such has been its oath through four years of devastating war. It is sworn to kill all who oppose its designs, if such a result seems necessary to gain its ends; and the initiate pledges his own life to assist in murder, arson, robbery, and the carrying out of all its schemes, on his first introduction to its mysteries. Not a few of the sudden disappearances of people who will never be heard of more in this world, may be traced to the "Knights," provided the knowing ones would uncover some of their *tracks in the sand;* and they will be forced to answer for the death of ABRAHAM LINCOLN!

This order, whose history, when known, will entitle it to outrank all the secret political orders of Italy, in the enormity of its crimes, *still exists*—not only in the Northwest, but to an alarming extent throughout the North and South; and its leaders are now plotting fresh treason; at the same time are subscribing oaths of allegiance and making the loudest professions of loyalty, while its outlaws commit murder, arson, and robbery to administer to the wants of its exchequer. It works in secret within its "temples" and without; places its assassins in hiding to shoot and stab; applies the torch at midnight, when the innocent are wrapped in peaceful slumbers; waylays railway trains, to tumble them down embankments, by the displacement of the track; conceals torpedoes in coal heaps to explode in steamboat furnaces and hotels; and comes upon the solitary traveler unawares, to wrest from him his money and life.

Investigation has already indicated that this order originated the plot to assassinate ABRAHAM LINCOLN, and when such is proven to be the fact, *as it will be,* who will contend that *all* its members are not accessories? Who will say they are not all guilty of the murder, and that all should suffer the penalty of that crime? If not all guilty, or equally so, it is important *now* to know who of these Knights are innocent, and the degrees of guilt of the others. It is of the first importance to them personally, to show their skirts clear of bloodstains; for the vengeance of the people will be appeased for this crime without let or hindrance, fully and to the last resort; and the guilty will suffer, whatever their numbers, or positions.

It is shown that the programme of murder was arranged on an immense scale, and at least one hundred prominent personages were marked for sacrifice to the Moloch of Blood. There were one hundred armed assassins at Ford's Theatre on the night of the 14th of April, each ready to aim the deadly bullet at the life of a victim; and only through that Providence that stayed the hand of him who had promised to turn off the gas and leave the place in darkness, was such an event averted! Other murderers were engaged in similar scenes of blood at other localities in Washington; and will probably never be known how many hearts God struck with terror or remorse—how many failed through fear or lack of opportunity, that otherwise would have added their names to this black record. What, then, may reasonably be supposed as the extent of a conspiracy that employs so many agents to do its work? Too large, by far, for the safety of freemen; too powerful for evil to remain in power.

When the tidings of the assassination were made public throughout the land, a few in each locality were inconsiderate enough to express gratification at the calamity of the nation! Who were they? Of what class and antecedent? Many paid the penalty for their blasphemy with their lives, and few stopped to consider that the executioners were heedful of the old Mosaic law, that requires "a life for a life;" but history, in other times, will so wake up the record! They were part of a murderous gang—part of the machinery that worked it into action, and equally guilty with those who executed the bloody work.

In other localities, remote from telegraph stations, detailed reports of the great crime reached the people *too soon*, and in forms greatly exaggerated, involving the death of President, Vice-President, and every member of the Cabinet. It is useless to assume that in such neighborhoods something of the matter was not foreknown,—but by whom? Evidence is plentiful enough that the conspiracy was extensive, and that its moving spirits were of the North and South, in combination. The investigation and working up of the evidence is in charge of shrewd heads, who will do their work thoroughly. It is no longer a question whether the conspiracy will be traced to its real projectors and abettors, for the tangled skein is daily unraveling;—new developments transpire as rapidly as the scenes in a panorama;—each discovery adds a fresh link to the chain of evidence that is gathering around the accused, to hem them in beyond rescue; and it is known that none of the guilty ones can escape.

The lesson is dearly purchased, but should be heeded by all.

PLOT TO ASSASSINATE THE PRESIDENT.

Whether Jefferson Davis and other rebel leaders contrived, authorized, or openly approve the assassination of President Lincoln, is a question to which we can not give a direct answer. The evidence in the case is collateral, and illustrative rather than positive. When Preston S. Brooks, of South Carolina, assaulted and tried to murder Charles Sumner, we of the North said: The South will denounce that act as cowardly and infamous; but, on the contrary, the South by her newspapers and public men, without one exception, applauded it. Since that time, beside making war on the republic, the South has evinced its fiendish hatred of the North by the atrocities committed on our dead soldiers at Bull Run, by the massacres at Milliken's Bend and Fort Pillow, by the systematic cruelties inflicted on our prisoners, by the Alabama outrages, by the St. Albans' and other piracies on the border, by the hotel burning plots, and so far as threats went, there has been abundant evidence that assassination was deemed an equally legitimate and justifiable method of warfare. The advertisements and editorials, appearing repeatedly unrebuked in Southern papers, proposing rewards for the murder or kidnapping of Mr. Lincoln, show that the rebel leaders did not object to such schemes though they may not or may have incited them. About a year ago, a correspondent of the New York Tribune, who had for some time been on duty inside the war office at Richmond, and who afterwards escaped to Washington, sent to that paper some valuable and timely information. He wrote subsequently from Canada, disclosing and thereby preventing more than one scheme for a murderous foray across the border. He foretold the plot which culminated in New York, in the attempt to fire the hotels, and he revealed the particulars of a conspiracy to kidnap the President, which the following details will show to have been considered and approved by the rebel President, Secretary of State, and Secretary of War. We quote in full a passage from a letter published in the Tribune of March 19th, 1864:

"In a former communication I stated that a plan had been submitted to the rebel War Department by Margrave, who had been for a considerable time an emissary in the North, to kidnap President Lincoln and carry him to Richmond, or if it should be found impossible to escape with him to the Rebel lines, to assassinate him. Owing to a change in the position of the armies about this time, the plan proposed was rendered impracticable.

"In the early part of November, and only a few days before he was sent North, Margrave submitted another plan, the details of which may be interesting to the reader. To give the plan in minutiæ would occupy too much space, but a digest of it will prove quite intelligible.

"One hundred and fifty picked men were to go secretly North and take quarters in Washington, Georgetown, Baltimore and Alexandria, so as to be able to communicate daily with each other, and, upon a day fixed by their leader, were to assemble in Washington for the purpose of making the seizure. The President, it was claimed, could be easily seized at a private hour at the White House, or in going to, or returning from church, or on some other favorable occasion, and thrust into a carriage and driven off. The carriage was to be joined a few miles out of the city by twenty-five or thirty armed men on horseback. It was proposed to drive to Indian Point, about twenty-five miles south of Washington, on the Potomac—two or three relays of fleet horses being stationed on the way—where a boat was to be in waiting to cross the river, and land the captive a few miles south of Occoquan, when it would be an easy matter for his captors to work their way with him through the woods by night into the Rebel lines. To prevent pursuit, every bridge between Washington and Indian Point was to be mined beforehand, and blown up as soon as the captive and his captors had crossed. Huge trees were also to be ready cut and thrown across the road in various places, as soon as they had passed, by men stationed along for the purpose, who were afterward to separate and escape as best they could.

"The Secretary of War thought this scheme might succeed; but he doubted whether such a proceeding would be of a military character and justifiable under the laws of war. He promised, however, to consult the President and Mr. Benjamin; but what conclusion was arrived at I am unable with certainty to say. About a week, however, after the plan was submitted, and the same day that Margrave left for the North, I asked Mr. Wellford, who is familiar with all the secrets of the Department, if the plan had been adopted, and he answered, "You will see Old Abe here in the spring as sure as God." A few days afterward I was sent to Atlanta, and never returned to Richmond to hear about the matter.

"But this is not the only scheme by any means that has been devised for kidnapping our President. Last summer a club or society of wealthy citizens of Richmond was formed for the purpose of raising a fund for this object. Circulars were sent to trustworthy citizens in every other city and town in the Confederacy, inviting co-operation in the grand undertaking, and an immense sum of money was subscribed. The firm of Merry & Co., bankers in Richmond, subscribed $10,000, and Sumner & Arents, auctioneers, subscribed $5,000; and I have heard on good authority that there were several in the capital who subscribed even more liberally than the parties named, but who they were, I did not learn. One man of Charleston, South Carolina, whose name I have forgotten, subscribed $20,000. It was proposed, when all was ready, to obtain a furlough for Mosby, and make him leader of the enterprise.

"Whether these schemes have been abandoned, or whether the kidnappers are only awaiting a favorable opportunity to execute them, remains to be seen; but certain it is that too much caution cannot be observed by the President, or the military commanders stationed at the capital."

As these statements were questioned by many journals in the North, the writer of the above subsequently forwarded to the same paper the following documentary evidence, being a letter from Calhoun Cullum, at that time a captain in a North Carolina regiment, and well known in the South. The original letter was sent enveloped, postmarked and stamped with a Confederate ten cent postage stamp, and addressed to Mr. Wellford, a clerk in the war office at Richmond. Although it was published as long ago as April 23d, 1864, its genuineness has never been denied nor its statements contradicted:

"MORGANTOWN, Sept. 30, 1863.

"MY DEAR WELLFORD: I have for several weeks been looking for a letter from you on the subject of our last conversation. On yesterday, Mr. Gaither, M. C. for the IXth District, came to see father and dined with us. He spent the week before last in Richmond, and had a number of conversations with the President, Secretary of War, and other officials. I inquired of him if he had heard anything of the *ruse de guerre* to capture "Honest Abe," and he said he had, but that the affair would probably be managed rather by individual enterprise than by the Government. He gave me the names of the most prominent workers in the project in Richmond, and as you must be acquainted with them all, I beg you to put in a timely word for me. If the affair was to be managed by the Government I knew your influence, and that of my other friends, with Mr. Seddon, would get me assigned to the part I desire to play in the grand comedy or tragedy, as the case may be; but if it is to be managed by the citizens of Richmond, my chances are not so good, and I may have to depend entirely on you. Speak a good word for me at once, and I will see you next week. As I told you, I would willingly sell my soul to the devil for the honor of playing a conspicuous part in the destruction of the *great hydra*.

"My arm is nearly well, and I find it quite useful again, as you will conclude from my being able to dispense with an amanuensis.

" Don't neglect me.
"Your sincere friend, CULLUM."

Now, it is remarkable that this kidnapping scheme is the same which Booth at first contemplated, as shown in his recently published letter, but which he subsequently abandoned for the assassination. If, then, one part of the plot of which Booth was the agent, was concocted at Richmond by Davis, Seddon and Benjamin, is it not like that they knew of the other part and of the more horrible shape which it finally took? There are unwritten chapters which will be unfolded to the public, as the trial of the chief conspirators progresses. There are chapters of such horrid detail and extensive combinations, that will startle the country equal to anything which has transpired since the commencement of the rebellion. The public have no idea of the extent to which the authorities have probed this plot. The accounts published give but a faint idea. They know the chief actor in the tragedy has been tracked and followed through Maryland, and hunted down in Virginia, and how he died like a dog; but this is only one portion of the whole affair—only one branch of the main stream which has been gone over. In almost every other respect, equal success crowned the efforts of the authorities; and in fact some instances, with much greater success, as the public will see in due course of time. The persons taken into custody as participators, aiders and abettors, or in some way accomplices to the tragic deed, are numbered almost by hundreds. There are still a few at large, and until they are captured it will not be the part of wisdom to give details and developments in full, which have transpired. It is but proper to state that the principal actors—the men, who, on the night of the fourteenth of April, were at their posts, and performed their allotted portion of the work—are in limbo.

The facts are not conclusive where the plot originated, but circumstances point strongly to its being the work of the fire-eating Southerners, who by their flaming speeches and boasts that a Brutus would arise to plant the dagger in the breast of the first anti-slavery President that was ever elected, gave the idea to their followers which has been put into practice by the over zealous fanatics in our midst who had not the courage, to enter the Southern armies, and fight for the cause which they pretended to uphold. Whether the detail or the employment of the leading men in the tragedy was the work of the rebel conspirators who had sought refuge in Canada or not the facts at the trial will no doubt tell. The fact that some of the parties connected with it were participators in the St. Albans' raid, and Confederates in the attempt to burn New York city last Fall furnishes strong circumstantial evidence, that the same brain that planned or instigated those atrocious deeds instigated and set in motion the plot for assassinating our late, lamented Chief Magistrate.

The conspirators were bound together by one of the strongest oaths ever taken by mortals and every person who was admitted to the secret, was bound to remain faithful to the end at the penalty of death—his life to be taken by one of his associates. Many of the Confederates were not taken fully into the secret, and those only were allowed to approach it who by degrees had their faithfulness tested. The authorities have been fortunate enough to ascertain where, when, and how often the conspirators held their meetings, and have taken into custody the people who occupied the houses where they met. The number which were taken into the secret before the consummation of the deed, was so large that it is astonishing that some one of the number did not reveal it.

It seems that about three weeks before the plans were put into execution, one of the parties revolted at the part of the work which the leaders had allotted to him on the eventful night, and at once manifested a desire to withdraw. He was, however, reminded of his oath and every effort made to bring him up to his work. But the more he thought of it the more he became alarmed at the fearful proposition of the hellish schemes. After several days parlying, he succeeded in getting the consent of his associates to relieve him from all further connection with them, on condition that he should leave the city and not return for sixty days. He left the city, and was somewhere within the limits of the Army of the Potomac, when the news came there of the Assassination of the President. He repaired immediately to Fortress Monroe and gave himself up and was sent to Washington, arriving there the next morning after the funeral services of Mr. Lincoln at the White House. When taken before the authorities he made a full confession of all he knew of the plot, as to where and when they met, and who were concerned in it. It is understood that the proclamation issued during that day by Secretary Stanton, offering an additional reward for Booth, also rewards for Atzerot and Harrold, was based upon the confession of this prisoner. At any rate the arrests on that day were numerous, and several residents of Washington were among the number. This opened the way for further important developments.

 The number engaged in executing the plot is very large. Besides Booth and his accomplices, in and around the theatre, the assassin of Mr. Seward, and Atzerot at the Kirkwood, there were a number engaged in cutting the telegraph wires leading from the War Department, and still another set endeavoring to divert the attention of the authorities from the fleeing culprits. It appears that at precisely ten minutes past ten there were twenty-two wires leading from the War Office in different directions, and connecting with the fortifications and out-posts cut. These wires having been cut at a considerable distance from each other, together with the simultaneousness of this work, shows very plainly that a number of men were engaged in it, and it is now believed that there were twenty-two men appointed to do this work. The time at which this was accomplished furnishes beyond a doubt, the hour which the President was assassinated, which has been stated all the way from half-past nine to half-past ten. It probably did not vary much from ten o'clock.

The numerous stories in reference to the contemplated assassination of all the leading officials in the government are not at all to be credited. The evidence thus far obtained, shows that the schemes only contemplated the assassination of the President, Vice-President and Secretary Seward,—no more and no less. For some reason the person who was to execute the programme on Mr. Johnson failed to do his work. Booth is the only man who carried out his part of the work to the letter. The would-be assassin of Mr. Seward no doubt considered that he had performed his work thoroughly, but providential circumstances prevented his blows being effective.

Justice bids fair to be swift in visiting these culprits and accomplices. The leader has already died a death of great agony and hard suffering. The future has confined within its unknown mysteries the fate of the rest.

THE ASSASSINS—THEIR PURSUIT AND CAPTURE.

The President and General Grant had been invited to attend Ford's theatre, in Washington, on the evening of the fourteenth, and both had accepted the invitation. General Grant was called North and left Washington during the evening. The President attended the theatre lest the audience might be entirely disappointed, in consequence of General Grant's absence. Shortly after the President and party entered the box and had become interested in the performance, John Wilkes Booth was seen, by one who knew him well, passing along the dress circle toward the President's box, when he came to within a step or two of the door of the box Booth stopped, and taking off his hat held it in his left hand, while he leaned against the wall behind him. In this attitude he remained for about half a minute, then stepping down one step he put his hand on the door and bent his knee against it; the door opened and Booth entered. The shot was the next thing, Booth stood upright with both hands raised, but at that moment no weapon or any thing else, in either hand was seen. He then sprang to the front of the box, laid his left hand on the railway, but was checked for an instant evidently by his coat or pants being caught in something,

JOHN WILKES BOOTH.

or being held back by somebody. A knife was now seen in his right hand, which he also laid upon the railing where he already had his left, and vaulted out. As his legs passed between the folds of the flags decorating the box, his spur, which he wore on the right heel, caught the drapery and brought it down, tearing a strip with it. When he let go the railing he still clutched the shining knife. He crouched as he fell, falling on one knee and putting forth both hands to help himself to recover an erect position, which he did with the rapidity and easy agility of an athlete. As he strode across the stage he shouted the motto of Virginia "*Sic semper tyrannis,*" flourishing his knife as he passed. When he reached the other side of the stage, just before he became invisible by passing into the entrance, he looked up and was heard to say, "I have done it," and was then lost sight of.

JOHN WILKES BOOTH.

It has been generally understood, and the family encouraged the belief, that Junius Brutus Booth, Sr., was legally married to the lady who passed in this country as his second wife. Indeed, when some seven years ago, the announcement of the death of the first wife, Mrs. Mary Booth, in Baltimore, was made in a New York paper, the statement that she had been divorced being added, the sons united in a card, which was published in that journal, setting forth that their father had had but one wife, and that one their mother, then (and now) living—the putative Mrs. Rosalie Booth, from whom he had never been divorced. This, however, was incorrect. The elder Booth was a married man at the time he last appeared at Covent Garden Theatre. While there, he chanced to meet in the Covent Garden Market, (then as well known as Haymarket) a flower-girl named Rosalie, who regularly sold flowers to market customers in that quarter of London. She possessed rare personal attractions, and was, in fact, exceedingly beautiful. Booth cultivated an acquaintance with her, which ripened into intimacy, and resulted in an elopement, Booth at once taking passage for America, where the fair Rosalie was presented as, and passed for, his wife. By his first wife, he had one child, at the time of his desertion from her—an infant. When she ascertained where Booth had gone, she also followed, bringing the child with her, and subsequently took up her residence in Baltimore. This child, when arrived at man's estate, adopted the profession of the law, and Richard Booth, Esq., was afterward known as a prominent member of the Boston bar. He never so much as recognized the other children of Booth, and for years did not speak to his father. It was probably out of consideration for this child, that the elder Booth did not sue for a writ of divorce from his wife Mary; if, indeed, there were any grounds upon which he could hope to obtain the desired legal severance, without which, it seems a second marriage was out of the question. Her troubles and trials led her gradually into habits of dissipation. She became almost as intemperate as Booth himself, and it was a custom with her, when in liquor, to haunt the Baltimore markets for a chance meeting with the woman who had usurped her place in the heart and home of her husband. These encounters were as much avoided by the one, as sought for by the other. Mrs. Booth assailed Rosalie with violent, often coarse language, opprobrious epithets, which the other never resented, but cut short by the speediest exit. The fact growing out of this condition of affairs is, that the children— Junius Brutus, Edwin Forrest, John Wilkes, Joseph and the sisters—are of illegitimate birth; and it is a fact which would probably have died out with the few who were privy to it, but for the great crime which has quickened public curiosity and unlocked the secrets of the family charnel-house, whose gates had been so securely closed and guarded by the children, in their struggle for professional rank and social position, that even a legal inquisition could hardly have forced them ajar. They were all greatly attached to their mother, and it was their custom, when fulfilling engagements throughout the country, to remit their funds to her in trust, except so much as was necessary to defray their personal expenses.

The elder Booth was an English tragedian, born in London in the year 1796. During his minority he played in several of the provincial English theatres with moderate success, and in 1814 made his debut at Covent Garden Theatre, in his native city as Richard III. His personal resemblance to "that hunch-backed toad" conformed so well to the stage-traditions, and his personification of the character was, in other respects so striking, that he at once took a prominent rank in his profession, and successfully competed with Edmund Kean, then the rising star of the English stage, at Drury Lane Theatre. He shortly after played with Kean at the Drury, and was subsequently announced to reappear at Covent Garden. Meantime an affair occurred which rendered him very unpopular with the public, and his reappearance was the signal for a serious theatrical riot, which resulted in driving him temporarily from the London stage. We do not distinctly recollect the particulars. Jealousy, professional or otherwise, stirred up the fiery nature of Booth and he attempted the life of the obnoxious person, but failed to take it. The man survived the assault, and is now we believe, a resident of St. Louis. Booth remained in England till about the year 1820, when he crossed the Atlantic, and made his first professional appearance in this country at Petersburg, Virginia, and the year following at the Park Threatre, New York, on both of which occasions he assumed his favorite role of "Richard III." From that time to the close of his life he fulfilled engagements in nearly, if not every theatre in the United States, and was accounted one of the greatest actors of his time, though the range of characters which he assumed was limited, and was confined almost exclusively to those which he had studied in the beginning of his career. Having secured a moderate competence, Booth purchased a property near Baltmore, known as "The Farm," where, during his latter years he resided, making occasional professional visits to other cities. He made an excursion to California somewhere about the year 1850, where he fulfilled a very lucrative engagement, and on his way home stopped in New Orleans, where he made his last appearance at the St. Charles, as Sir Giles Overreach, in "A New Way to Pay Old Debts." It was while on his passage from that city to Cincinnati that he died. His remains were taken to "The Farm" for burial.

Booth's habits were exceedingly irregular, and so interfered with his performances at times that an actor less gifted would have forfeited his popularity beyond redemption. It was rarely that he appeared sober on the stage, and, toward the close of his life, it required all the vigilance and art of managers to keep him in a condition to appear on the stage at all. The stories told of him in this connection are innumerable, and some of them extremely ludicrous. His appetite for liquor was absolutely voracious. Being without money at one time in New York, he went to a pawn broker's shop, literally pawned himself for money to purchase liquor, was regularly ticketed and exhibited in a window, where he staid till "redeemed" by a friend. On another occason, being announced to appear in Philadelphia — at the Walnut street, we believe—the manager, on the day for the performance, had Booth locked up, but was outwitted by the actor, who bribed the servant to bring a bottle of brandy, a saucer and a clay pipe. Inserting the pipe through the keyhole, with the bowl inverted, the brandy was poured into the saucer, and sucked up through the pipe by the thirsty tragedian, and the fact was disclosed when in the twilight the manager proceeded there to conduct him to the dressing-room, and found him in an insensible condition. It was considered somewhat perilous to play Richmond to Booth's Richard III, particularly if the actor was in liquor. During the combat on Bosworth field, he was apt, in his excitement, to consider himself in reality the King, and cut and thrust with the earnestness and ferocity of a man engaged in an earnest and life-depending trial of arms. At such times it was necessary to disable him, and it was in one of these "crazy spells" that his face was disfigured for life by an imperilled actor, the bridge of his nose being broken by the blow delivered through sheer defence.

The very ludicrous scene which occurred at a New York theatre, between Booth and the celebrated "fat girl," of Barnum's Museum, is probably familiar to many, and is, perhaps, one of the most amusing incidents in the annals of the stage. It is very doubtful whether Booth was insane at any time when not under the influence of strong drink. He was, however, of a very fiery quality, and in his peculiar sphere—the sudden and nervous expression of concentrated passion, as also in the more quiet and subtle passages of his delineations—he was, perhaps, unsurpassed by any actor of his time, and would have passed for crazy if it were supposed he was guided in his dramatic out-bursts by feeling rather than artistic skill. On the stage the elder Booth, was convivial, genial, warm-hearted, and as much loved in his profession as he was admired.

John Wilkes Booth—the infamous—was born on "the Farm," near Baltimore, Md., in 1838, and is consequently but twenty-seven years old. He made his first stage appearance in 1855, at Richmond, in "Richard III," at the St. Charles Theatre in Baltimore, and in the fall of 1857, appeared under the name of Wilkes at the Arch-street Theatre in Philadelphia where he played stock parts during the entire season. The name of Wilkes was given him by his father, in honor of an old Baltimore friend, Jim Wilkes, a successful merchant and great wit. Young Booth next became a member of the Richmond, Va., Theatre, improved rapidly in his profession, and became a great favorite there. During the season of 1860 and 1861 we find him engaged still further South, playing chiefly at Montgomery and Columbus, Ga. Probably not fancying conscription into the Southern Army, however much he favored the cause, he escaped North, and in 1861 and

1862 played in St. Louis, Louisville, and other western cities. It was during the season following, we believe, that he first appeared in Cincinnati, at Wood's Theatre, and left the impression, that though rather an unequal actor, as might be expected of one of his limited experience, he gave unmistakable evidence of dramatic talent. He had, added to his native genius, of a voice musically full and rich, a face almost classic in outline, features highly intellectual, a piercing black eye, capable of expressing the fiercest and the tenderest passion and emotion, and a commanding figure and impressive stage address. In his transitions from the quiet and reflective passages of a part too fierce and violent outbreaks of passion, his sudden and impetuous manner had in it something of that electrical force and power which made the elder Booth so celebrated, and called up afresh to the memory of men of the last generation, the presence, voice, and manner of his father. Convivial in his habits, sprightly and genial in conversation, John Wilkes made many acquaintances and friends among the young men of his own age in the city—an acquaintance that was renewed during two subsequent engagements.

Our recollection of Booth is somewhat indistinct; but we remember his features in repose had rather a sombre and melancholy cast; yet under agreeable influence or emotion, the expression was very animated and glowing. His hair, jet black and glossy, curled slightly, set off in due relief a high intellectual forehead and face full of intelligence. Both chin and nose were markedly prominent, and the firm set lips and lines about the mouth indicated firmness of will, decision, and resolution. He was scrupulously neat in his dress, and selected his habit with a rare perception of what was becoming to his figure and complexion. He would pass any where for a neatly, but not overly, dressed man of fashion.

Of his political views very little was known. He kept a still tongue on the subject, so far as we have heard. Being of Southern birth and education, it was presumed his sympathies tended in that direction; but he exhibited no particular warmth or zeal for the Rebellion, and nothing to indicate the remotest desire to further the cause by so much as giving it pecuniary aid, much less personal assistance. It is reported by a gentleman who heard the conversation, that during his engagement in Louisville in 1862, Booth fell into a controversy with the treasurer of the theatre—a rabid secessionist—while standing one morning in the box-office. He remarked in effect that he was a Southern man, and liked the people of the South, who had been kind to him, but he could not, for all that, admit that they had any right or occasion to secede; that they had it all their own way in Congress, and that if they insisted on fighting they should have taken the American flag and fought under that. There is another story, to the effect that Booth, while playing an engagement in Cleveland a year or more ago, asserted in a public bar-room that the man who would kill Abraham Lincoln would gain a more enviable notoriety than Washington himself. It is of course impossible to say whether these reported sayings are apocryphal or not.

The last appearance of Booth on the stage (except at one or two benefits in Washington), was at the Winter Garden, New York; and, in conjunction with his brothers, Edwin and Junius Brutus, in the play of "Julius Cæsar," for the benefit of the Shakespeare Monument Fund. He was, we believe, to have played with them again at the same theatre, on the 22d of April, for the benefit of the same fund. The play selected was "Romeo and Juliet", the cast of the Booths being—John Wilkes as Romeo, Edwin as Mercutio, and Junius as Friar Lawrence.

As the public journals have been and are still filled with paragraphs concerning Booth's connection with the oil business, it may prove interesting to learn that the War Department have thoroughly examined this matter, and the following are the facts established:

"J. Wilkes Booth never was in the oil regions of Pennsylvania but once, and that was last summer. He stayed two days at the Petroleum House in Oil City, and then started, as he said, for New York. He is traced to Salamanca and thence to Buffalo, whence it is supposed he went into Canada. He never purchased a single barrel of oil anywhere in the whole oil territory of this State, never purchased, owned or rented a lease, well, or parcel of ground in the State. Not a single oil company is yet found in which he ever held a single share or interest of any kind! Not a solitary individual can be found who ever sold him anything, or traded or bartered with him for anything in the oil regions. And the most singular circumstance is that not a single individual can be found in the oil regions of Pennsylvania who ever met Booth here and knew him at the time!

BOSTON CORBETT.

Boston Corbett, the hero of Booth's capture, was born in London, England. He was brought to New York by his father, at eigth years of age. He subsequently went to Boston, where he was baptized a member of the Methodist Church. He says, at that time desiring to lead a new life, he changed his former given name and was baptized "Boston." His subsequent residence has been in New York, when he enlisted in the 16th Cavalry. He is as modest as he is devoted, and his lieutenant pronounces him a most worthy soldier. He was offered one of Booth's pistols by the detectives as a momento of the occasion; but he declined it saying, he desired no reminder of the sad duty he had to perform, and desired to have it banished from his mind as soon as possible. He was recently offered one hundred dollars for his own pistol with which he killed Booth; but he instantly replied, "That is not mine—it belongs to the Government, and I would not sell it for any price." Being spoken to about the large reward, he replied he desired no reward for having done what God made manifest to him, in answer to prayer, was his duty to do. He remarked, however, that if the Government wished to reward him, and would allow him to keep his little horse, when his term of service was over, it would be all he could wish.

PURSUIT AND CAPTURE.

The first traces of Booth were discovered by Col. Baker, who recently made the successful raid on the bounty jumpers and brokers of New York city. It appears that Booth's leg was fractured in jumping from the President's box. Upon mounting his horse he proceeded toward the lower counties of Maryland, after being joined by Harrold who was intimately acquainted with the swamps and hiding places of that region. At first, Booth scarcely noticed his leg; but after riding a few miles, the pain became so intense that he went to the house of Dr. Mudd, in Charles county, and had it set at 3 o'clock in the morning of Sunday, April 16th, the second day after the murder of the President. Dr. Mudd split Booth's boot open to get it off, and when he left the doctor gave him a pair of crutches, and it is supposed he left in an easterly direction from the neighborhood of Bryantown. They then reached Turner's, about five miles from Bryantown, and while taking some refreshments, the servant was sent to inform the neighbors of their presence, Booth having been recognized. They discovered the dilemma they were in, and seizing the food on the table, decamped and took refuge in the swamps and underbrush. Some lady in Maryland presented Booth with a buffalo robe which was consumed in the fire at Garrett's barn, in which he was captured. Col. Baker's force traced him to Dr. Mudd's house, and the doctor was arrested by the military, with one of Booth's boots in his possession, which had Booth's name in it. The doctor was immediately taken to Washington.

Learning that no traces of him could be found after his departure from the house of Dr. Mudd, near Port Tobacco, where his fractured leg was set, Col. Baker became satisfied that Booth must have crossed the Potomac and escaped into Virginia, at, or near, Aquia Creek. He therefore procured an order for General Hancock to furnish him twenty-six picked cavalrymen to act as an escort to his brother, Lieutenant Baker, and Lieutenant Colonel Conger, who were to conduct them upon a route which a careful consultation of the map of Virginia had indicated as the one most likely to be taken by Booth. They proceeded down the river to Belle Plain, in the steamer Ides, and thence disembarking, rode across to a point opposite Port Royal on the Rappahannock. Here was a scow ferry, and the ferryman was critically questioned as to the passage of any such party as Booth and Harrold. The Virginia ferryman could remember nothing of such persons; but while Lieutenant Baker was exhibiting Booth's photograph with the view of refreshing his memory, a darker colored but more loyal Virginian, employed as an assistant on the ferry, happened to see the photograph over the detective's shoulder, and instantly replied, "Yes, master, I knows dat man, I set um across de river t'other day, wid three oder men, in two hoss wagon." The white proprietor could remember nothing whatever, yet the trail was deemed good. At Port Royal they took the Bowling Green Road, and passed the farm house of the Garretts, which, being about a quarter of a mile from the road they passed, and rode on several miles. This was about 3 o'clock, A. M. They met another colored Virginian, however, and from him learned that a party, such as was inquired for, was left at Mr. Garrett's two days before, by two rebel officers. The party then wheeled and returned to Garrett's house. Lieutenant Baker dismounted and demanded admittance and the surrender of Booth. The senior Garrett denied all knowledge of Booth; but seeing Baker manipulate his revolver, bethought him of two Confederate soldiers who had been stopping at his house, one of whom was wounded. He pretended he knew nothing of their names; he said they had been apprised that the Union cavalry was about and had left the house, demanding his horses and saying they must get away; but he (Garrett) stoutly refused to let his horses go, fearing, he said, he should never get them again. So Booth and Harrold fled to the barn, and Garrett sent his son to watch the barn to see that they did not steal the horses, and that he was at that moment hiding in the corn-house adjoining the barn. This was found to be as stated. Lieutenant Baker then went to the barn door and knocked heavily with his revolver upon the door, shouting out, "Booth, Booth." After a protracted silence, Baker continued the knocking and calling—Booth came to the door and asked, "Who are you, and what do you want? Are you Confederate or Yankee?" Baker replied, giving his name, when Booth declared he would shoot the first man who attempted to enter the barn.

When challenged to come out and surrender, he, in a very wild and excited tone, demanded to know who they supposed him to be and by what authority, desiring to know of what crime he was charged, and evincing the greatest excitement and talking very incoherently. The officers demanded him to come forth and give himself up. He refused to do so and threatened to shoot whoever should approach. He said he was alone there, but he would never surrender. Sergeant Boston Corbett was stationed at a corner of the barn where there was a board off, and where he was exposed to Booth's fire. He expressed a desire to go in and secure him, saying he was willing to venture his life in the encounter and had much rather go in and attack him than to stand in his exposed position; but it was so evident that Booth meant to sell his life as dearly as possible, that Lieutenant Doherty would not permit him to enter. The officers then gave Booth five minutes to surrender or else the barn would be fired. Nearly a half hour was consumed in the parley, however, when fire was set to the barn. During the progress of the flames Booth was seen by Corbett, aiming his Spencer carbine at one of the men. Corbett, who is a deeply religious man, says he prayed fervently for Booth, and that God would have mercy upon his soul, and feeling that he was justified in shooting him to prevent the possible death of another innocent man, approached the crack in the barn leveled his revolver and fired. His shot, by a strange coincidence, entered his head in almost precisely the same spot that President Lincoln was shot; the ball passed through and out of the upper part of the neck on the opposite side. Booth instantly fell, and his carbine dropped heavily with him. He was standing at the time supported by a crutch.; his body was immediately removed from the burning barn. This took place just at daybreak of the 26th of April, and he lived till almost seven o'clock.

Booth and Harrold reached Garrett's on the 24th, Booth walking on crutches. A party of four or five accompanied them who spoke of Booth as a wounded Marylander on his way home, and that they wished to leave him there a short time, and they would take him away by the 26th. Booth limped somewhat and walked on crutches about the place complaining of his ankle. He and Harrold regularly took their meals at the house, and both kept up appearances well. One day at the dinner table the conversation turned on the assassination of the President, when Booth denounced the crime in the strongest terms, saying that there was no punishment severe enough for the perpetrator. At another time, some one said in Booth's presence that rewards amounting to

$200,000 had been offered for Booth, and that he would like to catch him, when Booth replied, "Yes, it would be a good haul, but the amount will doubtless soon be increased to $500,000." The Garretts, who lived on the place, allege that they had no idea that these parties, Booth and Harrold, were any other than what their friends represented them —paroled Confederate soldiers on their way home. They also say, that when the cavalry appeared in that neighborhood and they heard they were looking for the assassins that they sent word to them that these two men were on the place. In other words they assert that they are entirely innocent of giving the assassins any aid and comfort, knowing them to be such.

Another account says, that the detachment of the 16th New York Cavalry under Lieutenant Doherty, numbering twenty-eight men and accompanied by two of Colonel Baker's detective force, which went down the river on Monday evening, obtained the first news of Booth at Port Royal on Tuesday evening, from an old man who stated that four men in company with a rebel captain, had crossed the Rappahannock a short time previous going in the direction of Bowling Green, and he added that the captain would probably be found in that place, as he was courting a lady there. On pushing on to Bowling Green the captain was found at the hotel and taken into custody. From him it was ascertained that Booth and Harrold were at the house of John & William Garrett, three miles back toward Port Royal, and about a quarter of a mile from the road passed over by the cavalry. In the meantime, it appears that Booth and Harrold applied to Garrett for horses to ride to Louisa Court House, but the latter fearing the horses would not be returned, refused to hire them notwithstanding the large sums offered. These circumstances, together with the re-criminations of Booth and Harrold, each charging the other with the responsibility of their difficulties, had aroused the suspicions of the Garrett brothers who urged Booth and Harrold to leave lest they (the Garretts) should get into trouble with the cavalry. This Booth refused to do without a horse, and the two men retired to a barn the door of which, after they had entered Garrett locked, and remained himself on guard in a neighboring corn-crib, as he states, to prevent the horses from being taken and ridden off in the night by Booth and Harrold. Upon the approach of the cavalry from Bowling Green, about three o'clock on Wednesday morning, the Garretts came out of the corn-crib to meet them, and in answer to their inquiries directed them to the barn. Booth was at once summoned to surrender but refused. Harrold expressed his willingness to give himself up but was overruled by Booth for some time; he finally surrendered, leaving Booth in the barn. The latter then assuming a defiant air called out to know the commanding officer, and proposed to him that his men should be drawn up at fifty yards distance, when he would come out and fight them. After the barn had been burning three quarters of an hour, and when the roof was about falling in Booth who had been standing with a revolver in one hand and a carbine resting on the floor made a demonstration as if to break through the guard and escape. To prevent this Sergeant Corbutt fired intending to hit Booth in the shoulder so as to cripple him. The ball however, struck a little too high, and entered the neck, resulting fatally as before stated. In his leather belt which he wore, was found the dirk which he so tragically brandished upon the stage, with clotted blood dried upon its blade. This knife, his carbine and two revolvers which he also had upon his person, holding one in each hand at the time of being shot, and while aiming his carbine, were all taken to Washington with his body.

Booth's confederate and companion Harrold came out of the barn at the first fire in an excited state of fright and professed contrition with his arms upraised. He also audibly besought Booth to surrender, without avail however. Booth in his forced hauteur shouted out just before Harrold left him, "Here captain is one man who wants to surrender mighty bad." He had but a moment previous insisted that no one was in the barn with him. Harrold is pronounced a mean cowardly boy. He said he wished J. Wilkes Booth had been dead before he had ever seen him, and then remarked with a silly tone and action, "He always liked Mr. Lincoln and was very fond of his jokes." Harrold was taken to Washington and confined among the other prisoners.

Booth, before he died, was apparently rational, but talked at random, and contradicted himself as he had done throughout, and said, "Tell my Mother, I have died for my country. You gentlemen have spoiled my fun in Mexico." He seemed conscious of the near approach of death, but died as frivilous and hardened as he had lived. His body was fully identified by his initials on his hand, in India ink—his memorandum books and other papers, and by the personal recognition, before and after death, of the detective officers who knew him. He had his moustache shaved off and had a uniform beard of four or five days. He wore a gray woolen shirt; had on dark cassimere pants; one cavalry or theatre top boot which drew up above the knee, but was turned down when captured. On the other foot he had an old shoe. His leg was bandaged where it was broken. Harrold said Booth had a third revolver which was burned up in the barn. Booth wanted to know where they would take him if he would give himself up. He was informed by the detectives that he must make an unconditional surrender. He is said to have showered imprecations upon his confederates, who, he said, had promised to stand by him but had all deserted him.

Booth was brought to the house of Mr. Garrett by a Confederate Captain, who told Mr. Garrett that he was a Marylander who was endeavoring to make his way to Johnston's army. Several small squads of rebel cavalry were seen hovering about, and were no doubt attempting to cover his escape.

Booth had $105 in greenbacks, and sundry Canadian bills of exchange, dated last October. His hair was badly matted —his clothing soiled—and the body looked more like that of a dirt bearer than that of the whilom fop.

Harrold said he was outside the theatre on horse back, awaiting Booth's coming out, on the night of the murder —that some how Booth got out and passed him without his seeing him, and that he galloped four miles across the Anacosta bridge, before he overtook Booth. He said Booth injured his leg by jumping on the stage and not by falling off his horse—that they changed their intended course and rode directly to the house of Dr. Mudd, near

Port Tobacco, to have his leg cared for; but they secreted themselves thereabout several days—saw the scouts pass and re-pass, and finally got across the Potomac by paying three hundred dollars for an old scow. Booth and Harrold narrowly escaped capture on the Maryland side of the Potomac. Marshal Murray and a posse of New York detectives, tracked them to within a short distance of Swain Point; but the Marshal being unacquainted with the country, and without a guide, during the darkness of the night, took the wrong road, and before he could regain the trail, Booth and Harrold succeeded in crossing the river to Virginia.

After the death of Booth, his body was placed in a cart and conveyed across to Belle Plain, to the steamer Ides, which awaited the return of the party, and brought to Washington. The two Garretts, who were paroled soldiers of Lee's army, and had just returned home, were brought up as prisoners also. Harrold, and Booth's body were safely lodged on a gunboat, at Washington, on the 27th of April, and the Garretts placed in the Old Capitol.

Surgeon General Barnes held an autopsy upon Booth's body, on the 27th. The smaller bone of his left leg was badly fractured—one of the smaller arteries ruptured—and the leg badly swollen. The ball entered the left side of the upper section of the neck, passing out on the opposite side.

ATTACK ON SECRETARY SEWARD.

Lewis Paine, the person who made the attempt on the life of Secretary Seward, gained admittance to the house by representing himself as one sent there with a prescription. When near the room in which Mr. Seward was lying, he was met by Frederick W. Seward, who demanded who he was and what he wanted; Payne made no reply, but striking him a blow with the butt of a pistol and cutting him with a knife, rushed into the room, he made his way to the bedside of Mr. Seward, who was lying on a low couch with his head inclined to the right. The thrusts of the knife were received in the cheek and neck. Mr. Seward's attendant came instantly to his aid, and the assailant thinking probably he had completed his work, grappled with him. The tussle was of some minutes duration, during which time the attendant received some very severe wounds. From loss of blood he sank to the floor, and Payne endeavored to escape. He was met at the door by Augustus H. Seward, whom he struck with his knife, inflicting a dangerous wound. His efforts to escape were further arrested, but he seems to have become inspired with desparation, and all who met him on his way out of the house, felt the keen edge of his blade.

Payne after leaving Mr. Seward's house, rode out of the

city with all possible speed. After going some distance he dismounted and disguising himself as best he could, returned to the city. Pretending to be a laboring man, and with a pick on his shoulder he proceeded to the residence of Mrs. Surratt. It was now nearly daylight and the officers had taken possession of the house.

Knocking at the door which was opened by an officer, he was admitted but was surprised and disconcerted at finding himself overpowered. His replies to questions put to him were incoherent, and satisfied the officers of his complicity in the murderous transactions of the night.

SKETCHES.

PAYNE.

Payne is shown to have been the confederate of Booth, and the one who assaulted with intent to kill Secretary Seward, Frederick W. Seward, Augustus H. Seward, Emerick N. Hansell and George F. Robinson. The antecedents of Payne are not known, and the first of him is his appearance at the house of Mrs. Surratt in the early part of March last, when he stated that his name was Wood. He called for John H. Surratt but in his absence he asked for Mrs. Surratt. He lodged there that night, taking his meals in his room, and departed the next day. About the same time he took a room in company with O'Laughlin in a boarding house in D street, where Booth visited them frequently. Here O'Laughlin and Payne remained about three weeks.

Afterwards Payne put up two or three days at Surratt's, where John H. Surratt, Atzeroth, Booth and himself had secret consultations. On this second visit Payne represented to some of the members of the family that he was a Baptist preacher. He and Surratt were found at one time in the bedroom playing with bowie knives. In this same room were two revolvers, and four sets of spurs similar to the revolvers and spur found in Atzeroth's room at the Kirkwood House. At another time just before the assassination he was found occupying a room at Herndon.

HARROLD.

Harrold is a young man less than twenty-five years of age, a native of Washington, formerly a druggist's clerk in that city, but for some months without any known means of support though during that time apparently well supplied with money He has frequently been in St. Mary's county, Maryland, always taking his gun with him. On the night of the assassination he was seen at the livery stable with Booth, and the evidence obtained before the court shows him to have been Booth's accomplice. It is shown by the evidence that he was several times discovered in secret meetings with Booth, Atzeroth and others of the conspiracy. He was found at Mrs. Surratt's in company with them. Accompanied by Surratt and Atzeroth he called at the tavern in Surrattsville and left the two carbines, the ammunition, &c., which were taken from that place by him and Booth on the night of the assassination. During their flight he acknowledged to Confederate soldiers that he and Booth were the assassins of the President. There is no doubt whatever of his guilt, and we trust he will suffer the penalty of his crime as it shall be defined by the commission.

ATZEROTH.

Atzeroth like Harrold is proven to have been a co-conspirator. He made his first appearance at Mrs. Surratt's in the early part of February, where he inquired for John H. Surratt or Mrs. Surratt, and was frequently found in secret communication with Booth and his confederates. To him was assigned the murder of President Johnson at the Kirkwood house. It does not appear however that he made any effort to get access to his intended victim on the evening of the 14th of April. On the morning of that day, he took a room at Kirkwood's, and was seen there at noon, and about six o'clock in the evening. He was traced there on horseback, but was not apparently about the house after that hour. He proved false to his confederates. He was active in his co-operation with them however throughout the night and fled at daylight the next morning; of his guilt there is not a shadow of doubt.

MRS. SURRATT.

This worthy, it appears, was cognizant of the intended crime almost from its inception, and became an active participant in every overt act. She was a general manager, and received and entertained at her house all the criminals except Dr. Mudd, O'Laughlin and Arnold. With Dr. Mudd she planned the means and assistance for the escape of the assassins. She visited Mudd at five o'clock on the day of the assassination, to see that the carbines, &c., should be in readiness and informed him that they would be called for that night. Booth frequently called at her house and had long interviews with her. He was with her in the afternoon of the fourteenth.

DR. MUDD.

Dr. Mudd's status is identical with the foregoing. Last November he is shown to have been in the confidence of Booth. He had a meeting with Surratt and Booth at the National Hotel in January. He introduced Booth to Surratt. Booth visited him at his room in the Pennsylvania House. When the assassins fled to his house he dressed Booth's wound and assisted in the escape of Booth and Harrold.

When the officers called at his house, Thursday after the assassination, he denied that he knew either of the criminals, and at the time of his arrest on the Friday following, he prevaricated, but finally admitted outright that he knew Booth. He says he first heard of the assassination on the Sunday after it was committed at church, and it is shown that he was in Bryantown on the preceding Saturday at the time when the excitement was at the highest pitch, the town guarded by soldiers, and every man, woman or child in the place had not only heard of the murder, but knew the name of the assassin. It remains to be seen what punishment the commission will inflict upon him.

SPANGLER.

Spangler does not appear to have been in the conspiracy at an earlier period than a few hours before the commission of the crime. If he be guilty his participation would seem to have been in preparing the means of escape by keeping the passage-way clear on the stage, and by closing the door after Booth had passed through, so as to retard the movements of pursuers. He knew the purpose of Booth, and promised a few minutes before the murder to help the assassin.

O'LAUGHLIN.

O'Laughlin is shown to have been in some kind of conspiracy with Booth. He was assigned to murder General Grant, but whether he failed through lack of courage or from disinclination does not appear. Atzeroth remarked the next day, when it had been reported that General Grant had been shot that "probably it is the fact if he was followed by the man that was to do it. It is said he withdrew from the conspiracy on Friday the day of the assassination.

ARNOLD.

Arnold it is stated quarrelled with Booth and withdrew from the conspiracy and went to Fortress Monroe, where he was prior to and on the fourteenth of April.

THE OBSEQUIES.

On the morning of the 15th of April, at half-past nine, the President's body was removed from the private residence opposite Ford's Theatre to the Executive Mansion, in a hearse and wrapped in the America flag. It was escorted by a small guard of cavalry. Gen. Augur and other military officers followed on foot.

A dense crowd accompanied the remains to the White House, where a military guard excluded the crowd, allowing none but persons of the household and personal friends of the deceased to enter the premises.

Flags over the Departments and throughout the city were at half mast. Scarcely any business was transacted anywhere, either on private or public account. Our citizens, without any preconcert whatever, draped their premises with festoons of mourning. The bells tolled mournfully, all was the deepest gloom and sadness. Strong men wept in the streets. The grief was wide-spread and deep, and in strange contrast to the joy that had been manifested over our recent military victories. That day was indeed a day of gloom.

The body was embalmed, with a view to its removal to Illinois, and laid out in the room known as the "guests' room," in the north-west wing of the White House. It was dressed in the suit of black clothes worn by him at his late inauguration. The catafalque upon which the body rested was placed in the south part of the east room, and was somewhat similar in style to that used on the occasion of the death of President Harrison.

THE FUNERAL AT WASHINGTON.

On the 18th the obsequies of the late President, at the Executive Mansion, were of the most imposing and solemn character. The procession was very large, and in its line were many of the most eminent citizens of the republic, civil, military and naval, including President Johnson, General Grant, Vice Admiral Farragut, the members of the Cabinet, Senators, Representatives, Governors of States and numerous others of distinction. The Foreign Powers were also represented by their Ministers. The route of the procession was densely thronged by thousands of spectators. Not an incident occurred to mar the solemnity of the august spectacle.

The procession moved from the White House at 2 o'clock P. M., and so great was its length that when the van reached the Capital the rear was still at Willard's Hotel, nearly a mile long.

The military portion of the procession was swelled by various civic associations from Washington and other cities, and a large number of State delegations. New York, Pennsylvania, Massachusetts, Connecticut, New Hampshire, Ohio, Illinois, Indiana, Maryland, West Virginia, and several other States were represented by large delegations.

Officers of the army and navy occupied a prominent place in the procession, all wearing crape upon their arms and sword-hilts. Several colored associations were also represented, one of which bore a banner with the inscription, "we mourn our loss."

Death had fastened into the frozen face of the corpse all the character and idiosyncrasy of life. He had not changed one line of his grave grotesque countenance, nor smoothed out a single feature. The hue was rather bloodless and leaden; but he was always sallow. The dark eyebrows seemed abruptly arched; the beard, which will grow no more, was shaved close, save the tuft at the short, small chin. The mouth was shut, like that of one who had put the foot down firm, and so were the eyes, which looked as calm as slumber. The collar was short and awkward, turned over the stiff elastic cravat, and whatever energy or humor or tender gravity marked the living face was hardened into pulseless outline. No corpse in the world was better prepared according to appearances. The white satin around it reflected sufficient light upon the face to show us that death was really there; but there were sweet roses and early magnolias, and the balmiest of lillies strewn around, as if the flowers had begun to bloom even upon his coffin. There was then no blood in the body; it was drained by the jugular vein and sacredly preserved, and through a cutting on the inside of the thigh the empty blood vessels were charged with a chemical preparation which hardened to the consistence of stone. The long and bony body was hard and stiff, so that it could not be moved any more than the arms or legs of a statue. It had undergone many changes,

Close by the corpse sat the relatives of the deceased; plain, honest, hardy people, typical as much of the simplicity of our institutions as of Mr. Lincoln's self-made eminence. No blood relations of Mr. Lincoln were to be found. It is a singular evidence of the poverty of his origin, and therefore of his exceeding good report, that, excepting his immediate family, none answering to his name could be discovered. Mrs. Lincoln's relatives, however, were present in some force. Dr. Lyman Beecher Todd, General John B. S. Todd, C. M. Smith, Esq., and Mr. N. W. Edwards, the late President's brother-in-law. Plain, self-made people were here and were sincerely affected. Captain Robert Lincoln sat during the services with his face in his handkerchief weeping quietly, and little Thad, his face red and heated, cried as if his heart would break. Mrs. Lincoln, weak, worn and nervous, did not enter the east room nor follow the remains. She was the chief magistrate's wife the day before; then a widow bearing only an immortal name. Among the neighbors of the late President, who came from afar to pay respect to his remains, was one old gentleman from Richmond. He had been hot in wrangle upon the boat with some officers who advised the execution of all rebel leaders. This the old man opposed, when the feeling against him became so intense that he was compelled to retire. He counselled mercy, good faith and forgiveness. That day the men who had called him a traitor, saw him among the family mourners, bent with grief. All these were waiting in solemn lines, standing erect, with a space of several feet between them and the coffin, and there was no bustle nor unseemly curiosity.

THE CAPTURE OF BOOTH.

But the first accession of force was that of the clergy, sixty in number. They were devout looking men, darkly attired, coming from all the neighboring cities to represent every denomination. Five years ago these were wrangling over slavery as a theological question, and at the beginning of the war it was hard, in many of their bodies, to carry loyal resolutions. Then there were there such sincere mourners, as Robert Pattison, of the Methodist church, who passed much of his life among slaves and masters. He and the rest had come to believe that the President was wise and right, and follow him to his grave, as the apostles did the interred on calvary. All these retired to the south end of the room, facing the feet of the corpse, and stood there silently waiting for the coming of others. Very soon this east room was filled with the representative intelligence of the entire nation. The governors of States stood on the dais next to the head of the coffin, with the various features of Curtin, Brough, Fenton, Stone, Oglesby and Ingraham. Behind them were the Mayors and Councilmen of many towns paying their last respects to the representative of the source of all municipal freedom. To their left were the corporate officers of Washington.

Still further down the steps and closer to the catafalque rested the manly features of Augur, whose blood has trickled forth upon the field of battle; the open, almost beardless contour of Halleck, who has often talked of sieges and campaigns with that homely gentleman who was going to the grave. There were many more bright stars twinkling in contiguous shoulder bars, but sitting in a chair upon the beflowered carpet was Ulysses Grant, who has lived a century in the previous three weeks, and came that day to add the lustre of his iron face to that thrilling and saddened picture. He wore white gloves and sash, and was swarthy, nervous and almost tearful, his feet crossed, his square, receding head turning now here, now there, his treble constellation blazing upon the left shoulder only, but hidden on the right, and one could read upon his compact features the indurate and obstinate will to fight, on the line he has selected, the honor of the country through any peril, as if he had sworn it by the slain man's bier, his state-fellow, patron and friend. Here also was the thin haired, conical head of Farragut, close by General Grant, with many naval heroes close behind, storm beaten, and every inch Americans in thought and physiognomy.

But nearer down, and just opposite the catafalque, so that it was perpendicular to the direction of vision, stood the central powers of our Government—its President and counsellors. President Johnson facing the middle of the coffin, upon the lowest step. His hands were crossed upon his breast, his dark clothing just revealing his plaited shirt, and upon his full, plethoric, shaven face, broad and severely compact, two telling grey eyes rested under a thoughtful brow, whose turning hair is straight and smooth. Beside him were Vice-President Hamlin, whom he succeeded; and ex-Governor King, his most intimate friend, who lends to the ruling severity of the place a half Falstaffian episode. The Cabinet were behind, as if arranged for a daguerreotypist. Stanton, short and quicksilvery, in long goatee and glasses, in stunted contrast to the tall and snow-tipped shape of Mr. Wells. With the rest, practical and attentive, and at their side, was Secretary Chase, high, dignified and handsome, with folded arms, listening, but undemonstrative, a half foot higher than any spectator, and dividing with Charles Sumner, who was near by, the preference for manly beauty in age. With Mr. Chase were other justices of the Supreme Court, and to their left, near the feet of the corpse, were the revered Senators, representing the oldest and newest States—splendid faces, a little worn with earlier and later toils, backed up by the high, classic features of Col. Forney. Beyond, were the representatives and leading officials of the various departments, with a few odd folks, like George Francis Train, exquisite as ever, and, for this time only, with nothing to say—not a whisper, not a footfall—only the collected nation looked with awed hearts upon eminent death.

At 12:10 amid profound silence, the Rev Dr. Gurley approached the head of the catafalque, announced the order of the religious service, when Dr. Hall, Episcopalian, read a portion of the Scriptures, according to the form of that Church.

THE OPENING PRAYER.

The opening prayer was made by Bishop Simpson, Methodist Episcopalian, who in the course of it, said that in the hands of God were the issues of life and death. Our sins had called for his wrath to descend upon us as individuals, and as a community. For the sake of our Blessed Redeemer, forgiveness was asked for all our transgressions, and that all our iniquities may be washed away, while we bow under this sad bereavement which has caused a wide spread gloom not only in this circle but over the entire land, an invocation was made that all might submit to God's holy will.

Thanks were returned for the gift of such a man as our Heavenly Father had just taken from us, and for the many virtues which distinguished all his transactions; for the integrity, honesty and transparency of character bestowed upon him, and for having given him counselors to guide our nation through periods of unprecedent sorrow. He was permitted to live to behold the breaking of the clouds which overhung our national sky, and the disentegration of the Rebellion. Going up the mount he beheld the land of promise, with its beauty and happiness and the glorious destiny reserved for us as a nation. Thanks were also returned that his arm was strengthened and wisdom and firmness given to his heart to pen a declaration of Emancipation, by which were broken the chains of millions of the human race. God be thanked that the assassin who struck down the Chief Magistrate had not the hand to again bind the suffering and oppressed. The name of the beloved dead would ever be identified with all that is great and glorious with humanity on earth. God grant that all who stand here intrusted with the administration of public affairs, may have the power, strength and wisdom to complete the work of his servant so gloriously begun; and may the successor of the deceased President not bear the sword in vain. God grant that strength may be given to him and to our military to perfect victory and to complete the contest now nearly closed. May the spirit of rebellion soon pass away. May the last vestige of Slavery, which caused the Rebellion, be driven from our land. God grant that the sun may shine on a free people, from the Atlantic to the Pacific, and from the lakes to the Gulf. May he not only safely lead us through the struggle, but give us peace with all nations of the earth; give us hearts to deal justly with them, and give them hearts to deal justly with us, so that universal peace may reign on earth. We raise our hearts to Thee to plead that Thy blessing may descend on the family of the deceased. God bless the weeping widow in her broken-heartedness; she bows under a sad stroke, more than she can bear. Encircle her in thine own arms. God be graciously with the children left behind him. Endow his sons with wisdom. From on high endow them with great usefulness. May they appreciate the patriotic example and virtues of their Father, and walk in his footsteps. We pray Thee, the Bishop said, to make the assassination of personal profit to our hearts, while by the remains of the deceased, whom we had called a friend. Do Thou grant us grace and repentance of our sins, so that at the end of life we may be gathered where assassins are not found, where sorrow and sickness never come, but all gather in peace and love around the Father's throne and glory. We pray Thee that our Republic may be made the stronger for this blow, while here we pledge ourselves to set our faces as a flint against every form of opposition which may rise up for its destruction; so that we, the children, may enjoy the blessed advantages of a Government delivered from our fathers. He concluded by repeating the Lord's Prayer.

DR. GURLEY'S SERMON.

The Rev. Dr. Gurley Presbyterian, and the President's own pastor, then delivered a sermon, standing on the step near the head of the coffin. He commenced by saying, we recognize and adore the sovereignty of Almighty God. His throne is in the Heavens, and His Kingdom ruleth over all. It was a cruel hand—the dark hand of the assassin—that smote our honored, wise and noble President, and filled the land with mourning. But above this hand there is another, which we must see and acknowledge. It is the chastening hand of a wise and faithful God. He gives us the bitter cup. We yield to the behest and drink the draught. This chastisement comes in a way heavy and mysteriously deep at a time when the Rebellion is passing away. The occasion has stricken down a man upon whom the people had learned to trust and upon whom, more than any other, they had centered their hopes for a restoration of union and return of harmony. In the midst of our rejoicing we needed this stroke, this discipline, and therefore God has sent it. Our affliction has not come forth from the dust nor from the ground. Beyond the act of assassination let us look to God, whose prerogative is to bring light out of darkness and good out of evil. He who has led us so well and prospered us so wonderfully during the last four years of anxiety and conflict, will not forsake us now. He may chasten but will not destroy. He may purify us in the furnace, but will not consume us. Let our principle anxiety now be that this new sorrow may be a sanctified sorrow, and induce us to give all we have to the cause of truth, justice, law, order, liberty and good government, and pure and undefiled religion.

Though weeping may endure for a night, joy cometh in the morning. Thank God that in spite of this temporary darkness the morning has began to dawn, the morning of a brighter day than our country has ever before seen. That day will come, and the death of a hundred Presidents and Cabinets cannot prevent it. The people confided in the late lamented President with a firm, and loving confidence which no other man has enjoyed since the days of Washington. He deserved it well, and deserved it all. He merited it by his character, by his acts, and by the whole tenor and tone and spirit of his life. He was wise, simple, sincere, plain and honest, truthful and just, benevolent and kind. His perceptions were quick and clear, his judgment was calm and accurate, and his purposes were good and pure. Beyond a question, always and everywhere, he aimed and endeavored to be right and to do right. His integrity was all prevading, all controlling, and incorruptible. He gave his personal consideration to all matters, whether great or small. How firmly and well he occupied his post and met its grave demands in seasons of trial and difficulty is known to you all, to the country and the world. He comprehended all the enormity of treason and rose to the full dignity of the occasion. He saw his duty as Chief Magistrate of a great and imperiled people, and leaned on the arm of Him who giveth power to the faint, and who increaseth strength. The Rev. Dr. Gurley, toward the close of his address said: I speak what I know, and testify what I have often heard him say, when I affirm that guidance and mercy were the prop on which he humbly and habitually leaned; that they were the best hope he had for himself and his country. Hence, when he was leaving his home in Illinois, and coming to the city to take his seat in the Executive chair of a disturbed and troubled nation, he said to the old and tried friends who gathered tearfully around him, and bade him farewell: "I leave with this request, pray for me." They did pray for him, and millions of others prayed, nor did they pray in vain. Their prayer was heard, and the answer appears in all his subsequent history. It shines forth with heavenly radience in the whole course and tenor of his administration, from its commencement to its close. God raised him up for a great and glorious mission, furnished him for his work and aided him in its accomplishment. Nor was it merely by strength of mind and honesty of heart, and purity and pertinacity of purpose that he furnished him. In addition to these things he gave him a calm and abiding confidence in the over-ruling Providence of God, and in the ultimate triumph of truth and righteousness. Through the power and blessing of God this confidence strengthened him in all his hours of anxiety and toil, and inspired him with calm and cheering hope, when others were inclined to despondency and gloom. Never shall I forget the emphasis and the deep emotion with which he said, in this very room, to a company of clergymen and others who called to pay him their respects, in the darkest days of our civil conflict:

"Gentlemen, my hope of success in this great and terrible struggle, rests on that immutable foundation—the justice and goodness of God; and when events are very threatening and prospects very dark, I still hope that in some way, which man cannot see, all will be well in the end, because our cause is just, and God is on our side."

Such was his sublime and holy faith, and it was an

anchor to his soul, both sure and steadfast. It made him firm and strong. It emboldened him in the pathway of duty, however rugged and perilous it might be. It made him valiant for the right, for the cause of God and humanity, and it held him in steady, patient and unswerving adherance to a policy of administration which he thought, and which we all now think, both God and humanity required him to adopt. We admired and loved him on many accounts, for strong and various reasons. We admired his childlike simplicity, his freedom from guile and deceit, his staunch and sterling integrity, his kind and forgiving temper, his industry and patience, his persistent, self-sacrificing devotion to all the duties of his eminent position, from the least to the greatest, his readiness to hear and consider the cause of the poor and humble, the suffering and oppressed, his charity toward those who questioned the correctness of his opinions and the wisdom of his policy; his wonderful skill in reconciling differences among the friends of the Union, leading them away from abstractions and inducing them to work together and harmoniously for the public weal; his true and enlarged philanthrophy that knew no distinction of color or race, but regarded all men as brethren and endowed alike by their Creator with certain inalienable rights, among which are life, liberty and the pursuit of happiness, his inflexible purpose that what freedom had gained in our terrible civil strife should never be lost, and that the end of the war should be the end of slavery, and, as a consequence, of Rebellion; his readiness to spend and to be spent for the attainment of such a triumph—a triumph the fruits of which should be as wide spreading as the earth, and as enduring as the sun; all these things commanded and fixed our admiration and the admiration of the world, and stamped upon his character and life the unmistakable impress of greatness. But more sublime than any or all of these, more holy and influential, more beautiful and strong and sustaining was his abiding confidence in God and the final triumph of truth and righteousness through him and for his sake. This was his noblest virtue, his grandest principle, the secret alike of his strength, his patience and his success. And this, it seems to me, after being near him steadily and with him often for more than four years, is the principle by which more than by any other "he being dead yet speaketh." Yes by his steady, enduring confidence in God and in the complete ultimate triumph of the cause of God, which is the cause of humanity, more than in any other way, does he now speak to us, and to the nation he loved and served so well. By this he speaks to his successor in office, and charges him to have faith in God; by this he speaks to the members of his Cabinet, the men with whom he counselled so often and was associated with so long, and he charges them to have faith in God; by this he speaks to all who occupy positions of influence and authority in these sad and troublesome times, and he charges them all to have faith in God; by these he speaks to this great people as they sit in sack-cloth to-day, and weep for him with a bitter wailing and refuse to be comforted, and he charges them to have faith in God. And by this he will speak through the ages, and to all rulers and people in every land, and his message to them will be: "Cling to liberty and right; battle for them; bleed for them; die for them, if need be, and have confidence in God." Oh! that the voice of this testimony may sink down into our hearts to day and every day, and into the hearts of the nation, and exert its appropriate influence upon our feelings, our faith, our patience, and our devotion to the cause now dearer to us than ever before, because consecrated by the blood of its most conspicuous defender, its wisest and most fondly trusted friend. He is dead, but the God in whom he trusted lives, and He can guide and strengthen his successor, as He guided and strengthened him. He is dead, but the memory of his virtues, of his wise and patriotic councils, and the labors of his calm and steady faith in God live, is precious, and will be a power for good in the country down to the end of time. He is dead, but the cause he so ardently loved, so ably, patiently, faithfully represented and defended, not for himself only, not for us only, but for all people in all their coming generations, till time shall be no more—that cause survives his fall, and will survive it. The light of its brightening prospects flashes cheeringly to-day at heart. The gloom occasioned by his death, and the language of God's united providences in telling us that though the friends of liberty die, Liberty itself is immortal. There is no assassin strong enough, and no weapon deadly enough to quench its inextinguishable life or arrest its onward march to the conquest and empire of the world.

This is our confidence, and this is our consolation as we meet and mourn to-day. Though our beloved President is slain, our beloved country is saved, and some sing of mercy as well as of judgment. Tears of gratitude mingle with those of sorrow, while there is also the dawning of a brighter, happier day upon our stricken and weary land. God be praised that our fallen chief lived long enough to see the day dawn, and the day-star of joy and peace arise upon the nation. He saw it and he was glad. Alas! alas! He only saw the dawn. When the sun has risen, full-orbed and glorious, and a happy, reunited people are rejoicing in its light, it will shine upon his grave, but that grave will be a precious and a consecrated spot. The friends of Liberty and the Union will repair to it in years and ages to come, to pronounce the memory of its occupant blessed, and gathering from his very ashes, and from the rehearsal of his deeds and virtues fresh incentives to patriotism, they will there renew their vows of fidelity to their country and their God.

The closing prayer, by Dr. Grey, Baptist, was sonorous and concise. He concluded as follows:

"God of the bereaved, comfort and sustain this mourning family. Bless the new Chief Magistrate. Let the mantle of his predecessor fall upon him. Bless the Secretary of State and his family. O God, if possible, according to thy will, spare their lives that they may render still important services to the country. Bless all members of the Cabinet. Endow them with wisdom from above. Bless the commanders in our army and navy, and all the brave defenders of the country. Give them continued success. Bless the embassadors from foreign courts, and give us peace with the nations of the earth. O God, let treason, that has deluged our land with blood, and desolated our country, and bereaved our homes, and filled them with widows and orphans, which has at length culminated in the assassination of the nation's chosen ruler—God of justice, and the avenger of the nation's wrong, let the work of treason cease, and let the guilty perpetrators of this horrible crime be arrested and brought to justice. O, hear the cry and the prayer, and the wail rising from the nation's smitten and crushed heart, and deliver us from the power of our enemy, and send speedy peace into all our borders, through Jesus Christ, our Lord, Amen."

The corpse was then removed to the hearse which was in front of the Executive Mansion, and at two o'clock the procession was formed. It took the line of Pennsylvania avenue. The streets were kept clear of all encumbrances; but the side-walks were densely lined with people from the White House to the Capitol, a distance of a mile and a half. The roofs, porticos and windows, and all elevated points were occupied by interested spectators. As the procession started, minute guns were fired near St. John's Church, the City Hall and the Capitol. The bells of all the Churches in the city and of the various engine houses were tolled.

First in the order of procession was a detachment of colored troops; then followed white regiments of infantry, and bodies of artillery and cavalry, navy, marine and army officers on foot; the pall-bearers in carriages next; the hearse drawn by six white horses, the coffin prominent to every beholder. The floor on which it rested was strewn with evergreens, and the coffin covered with white flowers. Then followed the President and Cabinet, the diplomatic corps, members of Congress, Governors of States, the delegations from various States, fire companies, civic associations, the clerks of the various departments, and others, all in order of procession, together with many public and private carriages, all closing up with a large number of colored men.

The nearest relatives of the late President's family there were the two sons of the deceased, namely: Captain Robert and Thaddeus Lincoln, N. W. Edwards and C. M. Smith, of Springfield, brothers-in-law of the late President, and Dr. Lyman B. Todd, of Lexington, Ky., and General and J. B. Todd, of Dakota, cousins of Mrs. Lincoln.

Mrs. Lincoln was not present at the funeral. It was said she had not even seen her husband's corpse since the morning of his death.

After the President's remains was placed on the catafalque, in the rotunda of the Capitol, Major General Meigs, Quartermaster General, remained until they were taken in charge by the guard of honor detailed for the night of the 19th and for the 20th, which was composed of the following army officers.

Brigadier General John P. Slough,
Brevet Brigadier General William Gamble, commanding 1st separate Brigade, 22d Army Corps, Fairfax Court House.
Captain R. C. Gale, A. A. G.
Surgeon F. W. Mead.
Surgeon Hard.
Captain Wickersham, R. A. G.
Captain H. C. Laurence, A. Q. M.
Captain Brown, A. A. G.
Lieutenant Gamble, A. D. C.
Lieutenant Pearson, A. D. C.
Lieutenant Moore, A. D. C.

NAVAL OFFICERS.

Lieutenant Commander Edward E. Stone, Monitor Moutauk.
Lieutenant Commander A. Ward Weaver, Monitor Mahopac.
Lieutenant N. H. Farquhar.
Lieutenant A. R. McNair.
Lieutenant B. F. Day.
Lieutenant E. M. Shepard.

A detachment of the Twenty-fourth regiment Veteran Reserves did guard duty at the entrance of the rotunda and at the gates of the Capitol.

As soon as the doors were thrown open on the morning of the 20th, the throng of visitors began to press forward. All were required to enter at the main eastern entrance, and passing in two lines on either side of the catafalque, to go to the western door of the rotunda. None were permitted to linger. A strong guard was placed across the lower steps of the eastern entrance, and a line of guards in close order on either side, marked the avenue left for the people who desired to pass in. About ten o'clock a heavy rain storm partially checked the crowd: but, notwithstanding the rain, the long and ceaseless procession of saddened faces came pressing forward at the rate of three thousand persons per hour.

The catafalque was better arranged to afford a view of the features of the honored dead than the one at the White House. The features were little changed, and by many are said to look more natural than when they lay in state at the White House.

The whole force of the Capitol Police, under the direction of Captain Newman, clad in mourning habiliments, were on duty preserving order, and politely, but in suppressed tones, and almost noiseless steps, directing the movements of the crowd.

The rotunda, which was lighted by only a sort of twilight hue, was filled with solemn stillness, unbroken save by the rustling of the dresses of the female mourners, and occasionally a deep sigh from some of those passing the coffin.

THE REMAINS OF THE PRESIDENT ENROUTE FROM WASHINGTON.

At 6 o'clock Friday Morning, April 21, the members of the Cabinet and many distinguished individuals met at the Rotunda to pay their last respects to the late Chief Magistrate. The Rev. Dr. Gurley offered up a fervent prayer, and at 7:40 the body was placed in a hearse, and followed to the depot by Lieut.-Gen. Grant and Staff, and Maj. B. B. French. Then came the Cabinet, consisting of Secretaries Stanton, Welles and Usher, Postmaster-General Dennison and Attorney-General Speed. The carriage of President Johnson following the carriage of Lieut.-Gen. Grant. On arriving at the depot, the coffin was placed in the car assigned. At precisely eight o'clock the train started, all standing with uncovered heads until the train passed out of view. The remains of little Willie Lincoln, who died in Washington February, 1862, accompany those of his father.

BALTIMORE.

The funeral cortege arrived at the Cowden Station of the Baltimore and Ohio Railroad Company, about 10 o'clock. Amid the tolling of the city bells and firing of minute guns from the forts, a procession composed of the military and civic societies, under command of Brigadier General Lockwood was soon formed, Provost Marshal Col. Woolley acting as Grand Marshal, and line of march taken to the Exchange, where the remains were laid in state in the Rotunda. The catafalque was richly draped, and ornamented with silver stars and fringe. The floor of the dais was bordered with evergreens and choice flowers. Upward of 10,000 persons viewed the body, but double that number were denied the coveted privilege, as when the hour of 2 o'clock, P. M. arrived, the coffin was closed and the remains escorted by the military to the depot of the Northern Central Railroad. At a few minutes past 3 o'clock the funeral train was wending its way to Harrisburg, Pa.

Upon reaching the State line at $5\frac{1}{2}$ o'clock, it was found that Gov. Curtin had arrived from Harrisburg in a special train, accompanied by his Staff. The greetings of the Governors of Pennsylvania and Maryland, was exceedingly cordial. At various places along the road the national banner was displayed, either festooned with crape or bearing a black border. The same solemnity of countenance was everywhere seen, and all seemed to be profoundly mournful spectators of the burial cortege. At York the ladies asked permission to lay on the coffin a wreath of flowers. The hand of affection could not have contributed a more choice and delicate tribute to departed worth.

HARRISBURG.

The funeral train reached Harrisburg at $8\frac{1}{2}$ o'clock, Friday Evening. It was heavily raining; but notwithstanding this the streets were densely thronged, and a large military escort accompanied the remains of the President, to the State House, amid the sound of minute guns, where the corpse was exposed to the view of the public until a late hour.

The train left for Philadelphia at 11 o'clock Saturday Morning. Thousands of persons were sad witnesses of its departure. The patriotic daughters laid a wreath of flowers on the President's coffin. The cars in quick succession passed country houses, workshops and settlements, every resident appearing to witness the passing train. Battle flags were displayed everywhere, banners were at half mast, badges of black were universal, and all elevated points, balconies, windows, housetops, &c., were occupied by persons of both sexes and all conditions, each countenance bespeaking a sad heart.

PHILADELPHIA.

The train arrived at the Broad Street Station at precisely half-past four o'clock, on Saturday afternoon, or two hours earlier than the schedule of time originally announced, in order to afford more daylight for the display. The military both white and black made a fine display. The city troop acted as body guard. In the procession were the Mayor, the City Councils, and other municipal authorities, Federal officers, army and navy officers stationed in the city and neighborhood, the Judiciary, members of the Legislature, members of Congress, representatives of Foreign Courts, and numerous others of distinction. The firemen and every society, institute and organization were well represented, especially the the Knights Templars, the Odd Fellows, and the Fenians. Many colored men also appeared as members of charitable and other societies, with appropriate badges and regalia. The chimes of St. Peter's and Christ Churches (Episcopal) were responded to by St. Mary's (Roman Catholic) Church. The procession occupied an hour and a half in passing the streets designated in the programme, when the Old State House having been reached, the corpse was taken into Independence Hall, where it was placed near the bell which first proclaimed the adoption of the Declaration of Independence. The Hall was clothed in such a manner as became the occasion, rendering the entire scene solemnly imposing. The houses were draped with mourning. Ingenuity was exhausted in showing to the best advantage this exterior manifestation of grief. The body of the President was visited by thousands during the night on invitation tickets from the Select Councils.

Before day light lines were formed east and west of Independence Hall, passing in by two stairways through the front windows, and out by the rear into the Square. By 10 o'clock these lines extended at least three miles, from the Delaware to the Schuylkill River, thousands occupying three or four hours before accomplishing their object of seeing the remains. Great numbers of women took position in the line, and notwithstanding the fatigue of slow progress, effected their object. Many, only giving up when they fainted, were carried off by their friends. The scenes at the hall were impressively solemn, and not a few persons were affected to tears. An old colored woman, 65 or 70 years of age, thrilled the spectators with her open expressions of grief. Gazing for a few moments on the face of the dead, she exclaimed, clasping her hands, while tears coursed down her withered cheeks: "Oh, Abraham Lincoln! Oh, he is dead! he is dead!" The sympathy and love expressed by this poor woman found a response in every heart, and seemed to increase, if possible, the general grief. It was not until long after midnight that the coffin-lid was replaced, and the face thus forever hid from the afflicted citizens. The Philadelphians did everything possible to show their respect for the distinguished deceased. The countenances of the people best express the sadness of their hearts. The good taste of the citizens of Philadelphia was displayed in the mourning habiliments of their dwellings and places of business. The ladies appeared with mourning badges on their left shoulders, and this custom was so general that its non-observance was noticed.

The funeral train left at 4 o'clock Monday morning for New York.

JERSEY CITY.

At 10 o'clock on Monday the vast crowds, which had gathered in front of the depot gates, were observed to surge from side to side, and immediately afterward the train moved slowly into the depot. It consisted of nine handsome cars. The car containing the coffin was large and roomy, black paneled, the upper portion festooned with black merino, looped with silver cords, with silver tassels drooping below, the whole surmounted with solemn rows of sable plumes. All heads were uncovered as the train moved in, and a most impressive silence prevailed throughout the vast multitude. While the train moved in, and for several moments afterward, while the remains were being borne from the boat the German singers, of whom we have already spoken, raised their grand and solemn requiem for the dead, until the vaulted roof of the great structure resounded to the impressive strains. In the interval, the crowds in the galleries remained perfectly hushed, and that grand song alone rose and fell, and swelled and wavered among them, like the lament of a mourning world.

The coffin inclosing the remains was slowly and carefully removed from the car and placed upon the stalwart shoulders of the guard which had accompanied it from Washington—a detachment of the Veteran Reserve Corps. The preliminary procession was then formed, and proceeded to the boat.

As the imposing procession moved through the densely crowded depot to the still more crowded street, and thence into the depot again, there was a most remarkable silence everywhere. The roofs of the buildings and the tops of cars in the company's yards were crowded to suffocation; the crowds in the streets were immense, and the same deeply respectful silence, the same breathless suspense prevailed throughout. Not the least touching feature in this display was that exhibited by the negroes, of whom there were a large number in the crowd. Upon their dusky faces could be seen the traces of grief, which sprang from instinct rather than from reason, a profound reverence which was worthy of the study of scholars learned in study of character, and of cause and and effect.

The hearse was a very handsome one,—a frame-work of glass, black paneled, inlaid with silver beads, with four nodding plumes of sable on either side. It was drawn by six handsome gray horses. The caparisons and everything connected with the hearse were simple, but appropriate and beautiful. After depositing their precious burden therein, the Guard of Honor marched as special guard to the remains, seven on each side—while the remainder of the cortege followed in due order.

The ferry boat New York, which was waiting to receive the procession, was appropriately decorated with flags and symbols of mourning. The bridge leading to the ferry was also handsomely decorated with flags and steamers, and the inevitable dead black.

After a short delay, the whole party were embarked, and the powerful steamer moved across the river with hardly any perceptible vibration, as if it were a thing of life and conscious of the precious nature of its charge. The requiem singers continued their solemn chorus. From far down the Bay came the echoes of the distant cannon, and nearer still they rang and reverberated over the boat. Guns boomed, the requiem rose and fell, vessels in the harbor dipped their flags in token of respect, and the hum of the peopled piers awaiting to receive their dead chieftain could be heard long before the vessel touched the landing.

NEW YORK.

The scenes at the foot of Desbrosses street was one never to be forgotten. Every foot of ground, every attainable perch, every house-roof was black, with human forms. Men and boys were perched on trees and telegraph poles; house-tops were so covered with spectators that it was a wonder that they did not fall in, and every window appeared to contain a dozen heads of eager spectators. But a strong force of police was on hand, and the best of order prevailed. Up the long open space, which stretched from the gates of the ferry-bridge, could be seen a clear, broad lane, awaiting the funeral cortege. The left hand hedge was the splendid front of our own 7th Regiment, as regularly formed as a line of palisades, the long line of policemen, on the right, presenting a no less creditable appearance. The arrangements had been perfected with singular judgment, and the excellent order which was everywhere preserved, notwithstanding the enormous crowd, reflected great credit upon the police authorities.

Indeed, we did not witness, in the entire march, a single disturbance of a serious character. The equanimity of the crowd, as a general thing, appeared to be equal to their respect for the departed President.

But little time was lost in preparations for the march to the City Hall. The hearse was first drawn out, the Seventh Regiment forming round it in hollow square. Four battalions of policemen, in excellent order followed, and the remainder of the procession came after in the same order we have already mentioned. A portion of the Washington delegation, however—that comprising the General officers—making the remainder of the march in coaches. Four policemen followed, and the remainder of the procession followed in the order we give above.

The appearance of the sidewalks and houses, as the procession moved up Desbrosses street, to the dull beat of the dead march from the band in the van, was most impressive.

Every window was full of heads, every house was covered with mourning, and the people on the sidewalks formed a solid, scarcely breathing wall.

Turning slowly up Desbrosses street, to Canal street, and thence eastward, the solemn procession swung down Broadway, to the same funeral step, the dense crowds gathering denser as they moved, while the most impressive silence prevailed.

On the procession moved amid serried masses of people ranged along the sidewalks, until it reached the City Park, and here words fail to convey an adequate idea of the impressive scene. Balconies, windows, housetops and door-steps, were crowded with fashionably dressed ladies and gentlemen. Every available post was occupied. Enthusiastic boys fixed themselves on railings, lamp-posts, &c., while in the Park many were perched on boughs and branches of the trees to the manifest peril of life and limb. The most perfect silence was observed, save at times, when a murmur of whispered grief, like the sound of distant waters, was borne on the air. Heads were uncovered, and tearful eyes turned heavenward as the remains of the martyred patriot—a nation's idol—were borne past. The Astor House was one mass of life, while the dark decorations of mourning waved sadly and sullenly from basement to roof. As the procession wheeled around the lower end of the Park the utmost efforts of a large and efficient force of police could not keep the crowd back. For a few moments the procession was broken, and outsiders had an opportunity of pushing onward to the City Hall to get a glimpse of the departed. Many were the congratulations on this point.

Anxious eyes looked out from the windows in the vicinity, while the crowd surged to and fro beneath. Rarely have scenes like this been witnessed. Death is at all times impressive, but under circumstances like these the feeling is too intensified for language to express it. The windows of French's Hotel were, like all others, full of anxious, eager, pallid faces. Moistened eyes rested on the funeral car which bore the last precious remains of a people's choice, and as the last honors were paid to the great departed a mournful silence pervaded the vast multitude. Never did the word of command, "present arms," fall on the ear with such a choking sensation. In the looks of those men thus arrayed there was something too deep for language, too overwhelming for outward expression.

The City Hall is reached. The coffin is removed from the hearse. Slowly and solemnly, with heads bent low, and look of profound emotion, while the bright sunshine glimmered on brilliant uniform and glittering sword, and waving flags almost darkened the air, the coffin is borne onward by fourteen orderlies past the military lines of the 7th Regiment N. Y. S. N. G.; past the veterans of the war of 1812; past the lines of the Metropolitan Police drawn up in hollow square—on, still on—up the steps of the City Hall, where one thousand German singers were stationed, whose mournful wail floated high above all other sounds, and was re-echoed within the dim and solemn chamber of the Hall, and borne onward beyond the military lines on the passing breeze to the distant, heaving crowd.

The remains were hardly deposited within the Hall when a column of eager applicants for admission was formed, which extended away through Chatham street, to nearly the Bowery. All races and all colors were represented in it, and we certainly never supposed that there was so much human patience in the world.

The scene in front of the City Hall was very animated. The long files of policemen were placed in a line running from the east to the west gate of the Park, and also on Printing-House square and Park-row.

In the Governor's room the decorations were beautiful. The portraits of the Governors and ex-Mayors of New York and the various other celebrities were all draped in the usual form of mourning. At 11 o'clock about 2,000 members of the Saengeround, Liederkranz and Arion Musical Societies marched in front of the City Hall and took their position on the esplanade, on either side of the main entrance to the building.

THE PROCESSION.

Even during all the night before, preliminaries for the great funeral procession had been going forward at many points in the city. Before dawn the stir increased. Almost as soon as it was light, the vast amount of our great metropolitan population began to move perceptibly toward the sadly magnificent ceremony of the day. At first many soldiers, uniformed and armed, or single civilians, in decent black, were gathering to a thousand rendezvous of regiment, society, club or association, as to centres of crystallization sprinkled over the extensive city map. And while uniform and civic costume varied in their respective many ways, two universal marks, distinguishable, indeed, in almost every citizen, whether to be participant or spectator of the sombre pageant—the crape badge on the arm, and the countenance serious and often sad—silently witnessed that the vast city arose in oneness of heart to offer a last testimony of grief and love at the death of the liberator, the patriot, the honest man and the wise ruler.

The procession formed in eight divisions. The first division standing in line for a mile and three-quarters on Broadway from the Park to Fourteenth street, could thus be conveniently followed by each of the others in its order, all crossing the Park and wheeling to the right into Broadway.

THE SPECTATORS.

As the time of starting approached, a tremendous crowd of spectators lined the whole of the appointed route, standing often in a dense human hedge twelve or fifteen feet deep along the curb-stones. Another almost equally numerous body occupied the steps, gratings and inner border of the walk; while all windows were filled with men, women and children—occupancy being often sold for money, and advertised by handbills posted up outside. Thousands and thousands of these lookers on were too young to know their right hands from their left, and were doubtless brought in order that, in old age, they might say they saw the funeral procession of Abraham Lincoln. Eaves, roofs, trees, posts, were edged or tipt or fructified with men or women. Along the middle of each sidewalk crept in either direction a sluggish, narrow stream of passengers.

At 1 o'clock, and with prompt good faith the great procession moved forward. The right of the first or military division resting on Fourteenth street, it was of course at that point that actual movement began.

THE MILITARY DIVISION.

According to a funeral etiquette, the order of the march as well as the position of the soldier's weapon, is reversed, and the last instead of the first brigade of a division, regiment of a brigade, &c., goes first. The Second Division of New York State troops precedes the First, the Eleventh Brigade precedes the Fifth, the Fifty-second Regiment is before the Forty-seventh, that before the Twenty-third, and so on.

Down the whole long line of the great thoroughfare, clear to the Park, the regiments were standing at ease, facing eastward. One after another, in quick succession, they turned into column of sections, and a bird's eye view would show the whole distance from Union Park to the City Hall, one long track of stony gray, bordered with the heavy black masses along each sidewalk, and from end to end, transversly striated with the sections, deliberately gliding northward in common time, the swords and bayonets sparkling and glinting in the perfect sunlight.

THE FUNERAL CAR.

The Seventh Regiment acted as guard of honor; and within its hollow square, rolling slowly nearer and nearer, came the funeral car, a gloomy and imposing structure, its heavy plumes nodding to and fro. Before the guard of honor marched a strong platoon of policemen, sweeping once more every inch of the street from curb to curb. There was, however, scarcely the least infringement of the orders in this matter. Here and there some weary old lady or careless boy sat down with feet in the gutter; but the crowd, though dense and massed to a degree even far beyond that of the remarkable occasion just after Inauguration Day, kept heedfully to the sidewalk.

THE GUARD OF HONOR,

the Seventh Regiment, Col. Emmons Clark, came next, with reversed arms; its mathematically accurate marching and thoroughly soldierlike array justified its employment in this melancholy but honorable duty.

The car itself rolled slowly and gloomily before us. Its sixteen gray horses were shrouded in black, and led each by a colored groom. Immediately about it marched the faithful squad of soldiers of the Veteran Reserves who accompanied the remains from Washington. The car itself consisted of a broad platform fourteen feet by eight, on which was a stage or dais where the coffin lay. Over this was a rich canopy upon four columns, having planted at the foot of each column three national flags festooned and craped. Above the four corners of the canopy were four great shadowing and waving masses of sable plumes, and at the top was a small model of a circular temple, unwalled, open, empty. Thus—so would teach this little emblem—was the nation, the home of freedom, bereft of its representative man. Or, perhaps, thus empty of its former tenant, was the body of the dead the temple of life. Within, the car was lined with white satin, and above the coffin hangs a large eagle, his wings outspread as if he hovered there, and carrying in his talons a wreath of laurel. All around the black draperies hung almost to the earth. Up on the surface of the dais and platform, beautiful white flowers were disposed in graceful, plenteous wreaths and boquets, and the deep blackness of the draperies is moreover somewhat relieved by festoons and spangles of silver bullion.

THE CIVILIAN PROCESSION.

The military portion of the processions is thus concluded, with a few small exceptions. With similar exceptions, the remainder of it, in place of the rich effects of the uniforms, the order of march, and the glitter and gleam of weapons, presented a monotonous, although impressive, column of civilians, in black clothes and hats. In several respects this portion of the procession was to the thoughtful observer more significant than the military part; but it was by virtue of implications and associated ideas, not by considerations of color and arrangement.

NATIONALITIES.

The numerical strength and watchful nationality of the Irish in New York was once more shown by the fact that one whole division, the Fifth, consisted entirely of Irish associations—and a large division it was. Among them marched, as in the Inauguration procession, a number of companies of boys, in green blouses, and hand in hand. The little fellows looked well and marched finely.

The athletic German turners, in their plain linen coats, looked strong, ready and sensible.

A long array of mechanics' protective and provident associations constituted the latter part of the civilians' procession, a very few among them here and there showing disgracefully enough, the influence of liquor.

The Brooklyn delegation constituted the Eighth Division, and after it, bringing up the rear, with a strong double rank of policemen before and behind, came a body of about two hundred colored men. Part of them were freedmen recently from slavery, and these bore a banner with two inscriptions: "Abraham Lincoln our Emancipator," and "To Millions of Freemen he Liberty gave." This was the only portion of the procession which was received with any demonstrations of applause. For them a just and kindly enthusiasm overrode the strict proprieties of the occasion, and handkerchiefs waved and voices cheered all along as they marched.

The head of the procession had reached the railroad station at 2:10. The rear of it had not reached Fourteenth street at 5. It must have contained full sixty thousand men. After the delivery of the remains to the charge of

BOSTON CORBETT.

the railroad authorities, it was hours before the rear of the procession ceased marching. The allotted route having been passed over, the various component parts quickly dispersed to their respective rendezvous.

The deep sobriety of this ceremony gave it a profound and weighty character, far more impressive than the festal pomp of most pageants. And the wailing notes of the dirges played by the bands greatly increased this effect. The streets were in remarkably good condition. The air and sky were perfect; the arrangements for the occasion very good indeed; and in grandeur of form, as well as in ethical and political meaning, the great funeral pageant given by the City of New York to the remains of President Lincoln was entirely successful.

THE CEREMONIES IN UNION SQUARE.

Shortly after the procession had passed through Union Square, Tuesday afternoon, a meeting was held for the purpose of rendering fitting testimonials of respect and reverence for the character of the late President, and joining in appropriate religious exercises.

Facing the Maison Doree, a large stand had been erected, with the national colors draped in black, and a broken column, the design of Mr. Thomas, round the base of which a roll of black crape was placed. In the square opposite the Spingler house and to the right of the stand, was a pedestal bearing a bust of President Lincoln, which is said to be a striking likeness. It was draped in mourning, and attracted much attention. In front of the stand about two thousand persons, among whom were a number of ladies, had collected, and the windows and doorways of the houses within sight and hearing distance of the stand were crowded.

On the stand were a large representation of the clergy, and deputations from the Union, New York, Century, Athenæum, City, Union League, Eclectic, and other clubs. A number of ladies and children were also admitted to the stand, which was most inconveniently crowded.

Hon. John A. King presided. The exercises were opened with prayer by Rev. Stephen H. Tyng, during which the assemblage remained uncovered. After repeating that beautiful portion of the burial service, commencing

"I am the resurrection and the life saith the Lord; he that believeth in me, though he were dead, yet shall he live; and whosoever liveth and believeth in me shall never die," the reverend gentleman said: "O God, in whose hands is our life, Thou hast pleased in thine infinite wisdom to take away the light of our eyes, the desire of the people; we bow to thy decree with submission, and we revere Thee as the high and lofty One. Thou hast chastened as a father chastened his children. We confess Thee as the Savior, we acknowledge the fulness of Thy power, we feel a thankfulness for that Thou hast given and now has taken away. We bless Thee that Thou hast made him the instrument of saving the nation, and proclaiming liberty to those in bondage. We feel a deep sense of our loss, but we bow in humble thankfulness for all our blessings. We implore Thee to bless the wounded and suffering, the widow and the fatherless; we implore Thee to bless and protect the new President, and to hasten the time when the nation shall desire war no more."

After the prayer, the band played the "Dead March."

Hon. George Bancroft then delivered a feeling oration. The delivery of the oration was frequently interrupted by applause.

Rev. Dr. Joseph P. Thompson was then introduced, and read President Lincoln's last inaugural address in a very impressive manner

This was followed by the reading, by Rev. W. H. Boole, of the 94th Psalm, which was pronounced by the inspired Psalmist against the enemies of his country.

Rev. Dr. Rogers then pronounced an eloquent prayer, in which he thanked God that our late President had been removed from among us without even a shadow on his name, and that a Joshua had been raised up to replace him.

After appropriate music by the band, Rev. Rabbi Isaacs, of the Broadway Synagogue, read a selection from the Scriptures and delivered a short prayer.

Rev. Dr. Samuel Osgood then read the following hymn, composed only a few hours previously, by Mr. W. C. Bryant:

> O, slow to smile and swift to spare,
> Gentle and merciful and just,
> Who in the fear of God did'st bear
> The sword of power, the nation's trust.
>
> In sorrow by thy bier we stand,
> Amid the woe that hushes all,
> And speak the anguish of a land
> That shook with horror at thy fall.
>
> Thy task is done, the bonds are free—
> We bear thee to an honored grave,
> Whose noblest monument shall be
> The broken fetters of the slave.

> Pure was thy life—its bloody close
> Hath placed thee with the sons of light,
> Among the noblest host of those
> Who perished in the cause of right.

Dr. Osgood also read the following composition of Mr Bryant, which he said had not yet been published:

HYMN.

"Thou hast put all things under His feet."

> O North, with all thy vales of green,
>   O South with all thy palms,
> From peopled towns, and fields between,
>   Uplift the voice of psalms;
> Raise, ancient East, the anthem high,
> And let the youthful West reply.
>
> Lo! in the clouds of heaven appears
>   God's well beloved Son;
> He brings a train of brighter years—
>   His Kingdom is begun:
> He comes a guilty world to bless
> With mercy, truth, and righteousness.
>
> O Father, haste the promised hour
>   When at his foot shall lie
> All rule, authority and power
>   Beneath the ample sky,
> When He shall reign from pole to pole,
> The Lord of every human soul.

Archbishop McClosky being unavoidably absent, the benediction was pronounced by Dr. Hitchcock, and the assemblage then dispersed.

FROM NEW YORK TO ALBANY.

The coffin was then removed to the train, the assemblage not leaving until it started. On the route to Albany all was in mourning, each place vieing with the other in rich decorations and mourning emblems; the people wore sad faces, indicative of their sad hearts. The train duly arrived at Albany, where the remains were exposed to view and viewed by thousands of people and thousands were disappointed.

The funeral train left Albany at 4 P. M., Wednesday, 26th. It was said that delegations from ten counties visited Albany to view the remains. The lying in state and the procession there had been marked by all the characteristics which had signalized the same in other cities. Special trains had brought thousands from towns not on the route to swell the population of the city. The houses were decorated with fitting emblems and fitting mottoes. The procession was beautifully ordered and very impressive. Gov. Fenton and staff were on foot immediately after the escort which left Washington, the latter in open carriages. At Schenectady, as always before, there was a still multitude with uncovered heads. At Canajoharie, the Palatine Bridge was clad in flags and mourning, and there was firing of guns, tolling of bells, music of bands, an assembled multitude. A refreshment car accompanied the train, and supper was had at St. Johnsville. The first young ladies of the town, dressed alike in black skirts and white bodices, with heavy black rosettes upon the left shoulder, waited upon the table and were afterward admitted to the hearse car and a view of the coffin. The ladies of Little Falls placed fresh flowers upon the coffin. At Herkimer blazing torches showed the train in a bright light to an immense company, who spoke not a word, but let him pass on in his glory. Multiplied thousands, made wierd by torches, met the train at Utica, with bells tolling and guns firing. It was estimated that 25,000 persons were present. Passing Oriskany, where the people had kindled a large bonfire, the train reached Syracuse at 11:15 P. M. The depot and other buildings were draped in mourning, and the scene was illuminated with locomotive lamps. A band of music played a dirge as the train entered the depot, and a choir of 100 voices sang appropriate hymns during the stoppage of the train. The crowd of citizens was immense, and large delegations came in from Oswego, and the surrounding towns. The train was received by the assembled multitude with uncovered heads, and with every manifestation of heartfelt sorrow. The way stations were illuminated with torches and bonfires. At midnight the train reached Memphis.

Thursday, April 27, the remains passed through, Jordon, Weedsport, Port Byron, Savannah, Clyde, Lyons, Newark, Palmyra, and other places where the crowds were very large, and the train moved past the stations in the light of countless bonfires and torches, arriving at Rochester at 3:20 A. M. The cortage stopped 10 minutes at Rochester. The people were abroad in full force. The streets in the vicinity of the stopping places were crowded. Houses were draped with the usual emblems and draped flags.

BUFFALO

was reached at 7 A. M. The procession was formed between 7 and 8 o'clock, and proceeded toward St. James Hall, under a civil and military escort, in company with the party which had followed the remains from Washington. The coffin was prominently in view of the very many persons who lined the streets through which the cortage passed. The hearse was heavily covered with black cloth, surmounted with an arched roof and tastefully trimmed with white satin and silver lace. The body was deposited, beneath a crape canopy in St. James Hall, a dirge being chanted in the mean time. An elegant harp of choice white flowers was then placed at the head of the coffin, and the public were admitted. The throng was immense until 8 P. M., when the coffin was closed. The arrangements generally were pronounced to be better than elsewhere on the route. At 10 P. M., the train left for

CLEVELAND.

At 21:10 A. M, Friday, the 28th, the train arrived at Dunkirk. The chief feature at that place was a group of 36 young ladies representing the States of the Union. They were dressed in white, each with a broad black scarf resting on the shoulder, and holding in the hand a National flag. The crowd here was dense. The tolling of bells, the solemn music of an instrumental band, and the firing of minute guns, contributed to the interest of the scene. Passing through Braceton, which was illuminated, the train reached Westfield at 1 A. M., where a committee of ladies brought in a cross and wreath of flowers: On the cross were the words: "Ours the cross; thine the crown." Soon after the train reached the state boundary, and General Dix and staff took leave of the funeral party. At Wiskliffe Governor Brough and staff, of Ohio, came on board; also Major Gen. Hooker and staff. The train arrived at Cleveland at 7 A. M. On the lake side of the city thousands of persons were gathered on the slooping green hillside, all having a good view of the train. High up was seen an arch with the inscription, "Abraham Lincoln." It was draped in mourning, and the supports were covered with alternate strips of black and white. The body was borne to the park, where a building had been erected especially for the reception of the remains. The building was 24 by 36 feet in dimensions, and 14 feet high from the ground to the plate. The roof was of pagoda style, and the rafters were covered with white cloth over the centre of the main roof, and directly over the catafalque a second roof was raised about four feet and covered in like manner. The catafalque consisted of a raised dias, and was ornamented with evergreens in the most beautiful manner. Silver-fringed drapery was looped to the columns supporting the canopy, the borders of the cornice being illuminated with white roses and stars of silver. The religious services, after the remains had been put on the dias, were performed by the Right Rev. Bishop McIlvaine. He read a part of the funeral service of the Episcopal Church, slightly altering the text to suit the occasion, and moved many of the listeners to tears. The remains were then exposed to public view. The arrangements were so perfect that every one who desired to see them had no difficulty; the number visiting them during the day averaging 180 per minute. At midnight on Friday, April 29th, the cortege left Cleveland, in a heavy rain, for Columbus. Notwithstanding the storm, groups of people were assembled at all the stations, many of them bearing lanterns in their hands, in order that the funeral train might be plainly seen. The largest gathering was at Condingham, at which place the buildings were handsomely draped, guns fired, and bells rung. At 6 A. M. the train passed Eden. The rain had ceased and the weather was clear.

COLUMBUS.

At 7½ A. M., Saturday, the 20th, the cortege arrived at Columbus. The Committee of Arrangements began at once to carry out the programme and place the funeral party in carriages. The procession was formed, the 38th Ohio Volunteer Infantry acting as a military escort: then followed the officiating clergy, pall-bearers and others, on each side of the hearse. The Veteran Reserve Corps were the guard of honor. The rotunda of the Capitol was draped in mourning. The coffin was approached by five steps. It rested on a mound of moss, in which were dotted the choicest flowers. At the head of the coffin rested a large floral wreath, while directly behind the latter were flowers in glass and china vessels, contributed by ladies. At the corners of the platform, on the floor, were large vases filled with flowers. The walls were adorned with a naval picture representing a scene in the life of Commodore Perry, and with various banners which had been carried by Ohio troops during the war, torn and riddled by bullets in many a deadly conflict. No confusion whatever was occasioned in entering and retiring from the Capitol, owing to the admirable arrangements, and for about seven hours there was a constant line of spectators passing before the remains. At 8 P. M. the remains were again conveyed to the train, and the funeral escort left for Indianapolis. Scioto, Hillard's, Pleasant Valley, Unionville, Milford, Woodstock and Vagdenburgh were passed, and along the road the people appeared to the number of thousands, carrying torches and kindling bonfires, to enable them clearly to see the funeral car. At Woodstock there was both instrumental and vocal music, and the tolling of bells and other manifestations of mourning. At Urbana the people were congregated by thousands. The scene was lit up with a hundred torches and bonfires, and the countenances of the interested multitude were seen in the lurid glare. Guns were fired and bells tolled, and there was music from an instrumental band, but the melody which charmed the most was from a choir of both males and females stationed upon the platform, who sang a deeply impressive hymn. At Piqua 10,000 persons were assembled.

Between 12 and 1 A. M., Sunday 30th, the State line was passed, and the train entered Indiana. The weather was cold, and the rain was again falling, but there was no diminuation in the crowd assembled at various points. At Richmond the train passed under an arched bridge constructed for the purpose by the Air Line Railroad. It had a span of 25 feet, and was 30 feet in height. The abutments were trimmed with evergreens dotted with white roses, and the mourning drapery in close association. At this point Gov. Morton of Indiana came on board. At Cambridge thousands of people were at the depot and the train passed under an arch trimmed with evergreens, surmounted by a female figure to represent the Genius of America weeping. The State of Indiana was plunged in the depth of grief. This was shown, not by the magnificent demonstrations in the cities and towns, but along the line the farm houses were decorated with mourning and their inmates gathered in clusters, and by the light of bonfires and torches caught glimpses of the train which was bearing from their sight the lamented Chief Magistrate.

INDIANAPOLIS.

The cortege arrived at Indianapolis at 7 A. M. A procession was formed, and through a throng of thousands of spectators the body of the dead President was borne to the State House. The entire structure was beautifully shrouded in black and white relieved by evergreen garlands, with a fine display of flags. The platform was in the centre of the rotunda. On this the coffin was placed, surrounded by flowers, while wreaths and floral crosses were laid upon the lid. The remains were soon after their arrival exposed to public view. The city Councils of Louisville and Cincinnati and a delegation from Covington, together with Governor Bramlette of Kentucky, were in the city to take part in the funeral procession. Thousands of persons from the surrounding country thronged the city. The Sabbath-School children were the first admitted, then the ladies and citizens severally passed through the hall from South to North.

At midnight of Sunday, the remains left Indianapolis for Chicago. The usual emblems of mourning were seen on the route. At Michigan City the train passed beneath a number of beautiful arches erected in memory of the honored dead. Soon afterward the boundry line was passed, and the cortege entered Illinois.

CHICAGO.

Chicago was reached at 11 o'clock, A. M., May 1st, the train having run 1,500 miles since leaving Washington. On the previous night the Hon. Scuyler Colfax delivered an eloquent funeral oration at Bryan Hall to an immense audience. Minute guns and tolling and chiming bells, announced the arrival of the President's remains. The remains of the President were conveyed to the Court House, which was opened to the public at 6 o'clock in the afternoon, and remained open till 7 o'clock P. M. of the next day, thousands of persons crowding thither to see for the last time the face of the lamented dead.

CHICAGO TO SPRINGFIELD.

The route to Springfield was one grand series of bonfires burning at every station, lighting up the darkness, and showing to advantage the train, as well as the decorated stands where stood the men and women. Many places had instrumental and vocal music, chanting dirges and performing requiems. The train reached Springfield about daylight, where an immense throng was gathered to witness the reception, etc.

SPRINGFIELD.

After placing the coffin in the hearse, the procession formed and proceeded to the Capitol, which had been highly adorned in every part for the occasion. The catafalque was built in the Hall of Representatives, which was festooned with rich mourning drapery, and had plants and flowers distributed in tasteful display. The canopy, beautiful in itself, was handsomely decorated in a style of magnificence unsurpassed by anything connected with the pageant from Washington through all of the cities. The ground and buildings were given in charge of Co. E, 23d Regiment Veteran Reserve Corps. About 10 o'clock A. M., May 2nd, the arrangements were completed and the people were admitted.

For twenty four hours the throng passed, even through the
night. May 3d, at 11 o'clock, the procession formed and
moved off toward Oak Ridge Cemetry. On the route the
band played "Dead March in Saul," with solemn and mournful effect. The gate of the cemetry was ornamented with
evergreens and flowers. The coffin being deposited in the
cemetery, the exercises were opened by Rev. A. Hull, in an
appropriate prayer, and a dirge followed. The Rev. N. W.
Miner then read choice selections from the books of St. John
and St. Paul; after which Rev. N. C. Hubbard read the
last inaugural of Mr. Lincoln. Bishop Simpson then arose
to deliver his address, to which all listened attentively and
gravely. He commenced as follows:

BISHOP SIMPSON'S ADDRESS.

*Fellow-citizens of Illinois and of many parts of our entire
Union, near the Capital of this large and growing State of
Illinois:*

In the midst of this beautiful grove, and at the open
mouth of this vault, which has just received the remains
of our fallen chieftain, we gather to pay a tribute of respect and to drop the tears of sorrow around the ashes of
the mighty dead. A little more than four years ago,
from his plain, quiet home in yonder city, he started, receiving
the parting words of the concourse of friends who gathered around him, and in the midst of the dropping of the
gentle shower, he told of the pangs of parting from the
place where his children had been born, and his home had
been made pleasant by early recollections; and as he left,
he made an earnest request, in the hearing of some who

are present at this meeting, that, as he was about to enter upon the responsibilities which he believed to be greater than any which had fallen upon any man since the days of Washington, the people would offer up prayers that God would aid and sustain him in the work which they had given him to do. His company left our quiet city, but as it went, snares were in waiting for the Chief Magistrate. Scarcely did he escape the dangers of the way, or the hands of the assassin as he neared Washington, and I believe he escaped only through the vigilance of officers and the prayers of his people, so that the blow was suspended for more than four years, which was at last permitted, through the providence of God, to fall. How different the occasion which witnessed his departure from that which witnessed his return! You expected to take him by the hand, to feel the warm grasp which you had felt in other days, and to see the tall form walking among you which you had delighted to honor in years past. But he was never permitted to return until he came with lips mute and silent, the frame encoffined, and a weeping nation followed as his mourners.

Such a scene as his return to you, was never witnessed among the events of history. There have been great processions of mourners. There was one for the Patriarch Jacob, which came up from Egypt, and the Egyptians wondered at the evidences of reverence and filial affection which came from the hearts of the Israelites. There was mourning when Moses fell upon the heights of Pisgah, and vanished from human view. There have been mournings in the kingdoms of the earth, when Kings and Princes have fallen; but never was there in the history of man such mourning as that which has accompanied this funeral procession, and has gathered around the mortal remains of him who was our loved one, and who now sleeps among us.

If we glance at the procession which followed him, we see how the nation stood aghast! Tears filled the eyes of manly, sun-burnt faces; strong men, as they clasped the hands of their friends, were unable to find vent for their grief in words. Women and children caught up the tidings as they ran through the land, and were melted into tears. The nation stood still, and men left their plows in the field and asked what the end should be. The hum of manufactories ceased, and the sound of the hammer was not heard. Busy merchants closed their doors, and in the Exchange gold passed no more from hand to hand. Though three weeks have passed, the nation has scarcely breathed easily yet. A mournful silence is abroad upon the land. Nor is this mourning confined to any class, or to any district of country. Men of all political parties, and of all religious creeds, have united in paying this mournful tribute. The Archbishop of the Roman Catholic Church, in New York, and a Protestant Minister, walked side by side in the sad procession, and a Jewish Rabbi performed a part of the solemn services.

There are gathered around this tomb the representatives of the army and navy, Senators, Judges, Governors, and officers of all the branches of the Government. Here, too, are all members of civic professions, with men and women from the humblest as well the highest occupations. Here and there, too, are tears as sincere and warm as any that drop, which come from the eyes of those whose kindred and whose race have been freed from their chains by him whom they mourn as their deliverer. Far more have gazed on the face of the departed than ever looked upon the face of any other departed man. More races have looked on the procession for 1,600 miles or more, by night and by day, by sunlight, dawn, twilight, and by torchlight, than ever before watched the progress of a procession.

We ask, why this wonderful mourning, this great procession? I answer, first, a part of the interest has arisen from the times in which we live, and in which he, that has fallen, was a principal actor. It is a principle of our nature that feeling once excited, readily leave the object by which they are excited for some other object, which may, for the time being, take possession of the mind. Another principle is, that the deepest affections of our hearts gather around some human form, in which are embodied the living thoughts and ideas of the passing ages. If we look, then, at the times we see an age of excitement. For four years the popular heart has been stirred to its utmost depths. War had come upon us, devouring families, separating nearest and dearest friends, a war, the extent and magnitude of which no one could estimate; a war in which the blood of brethren was shed by a brother's hand. A call for soldiers was made by this voice now hushed, and all over this land, from hill and mountain, from plain and valley, there sprung up hundreds of thousands of bold hearts, ready to go forth and save our national Union.

The feeling of excitement was transferred next into a

feeling of deep grief, because of the danger in which our country was placed. Many said, "Is it possible to save our nation?" Some in our country, and nearly all the leading men in other countries, declared it to be impossible to maintain the Union, and many an honest and patriotic heart was deeply pained with apprehensions of common ruin; and many in grief, and almost in despair, anxiously inquired, "What shall the end of these things be? In addition to this, wives had given their husbands, mothers their sons, the pride and joy of their hearts. They saw them put on the uniform—they saw them take the martial step, and they tried to hide their deep feeling of sadness. Many dear ones stepped upon the battle-field never to return again, and there was mourning in every mansion and in every cabin in our broad land.

Then came a feeling of deeper sadness, as the story came of prisoners tortured to death or starved, through the mandates of those who are called the representatives of chivalry, or who claim to be honorable ones of the earth; and as we read the stories of frames attenuated and reduced to mere skeletons, our grief turned partly into horror and partly into a cry for vengeance. Then this feeling was changed to one of joy. There came signs of the end of this rebellion. We followed the cue of our glorious Generals. We saw our army under the command of the brave officer who is guiding this procession, climb up the hights of Lookout Mountain and drive the rebels from their strongholds. Another brave General swept through Georgia, South and North Carolina, and drove the combined armies of the rebels before him, while the honored Lieutenant-General held Lee and his followers in a death-grasp.

Then the tidings came that Richmond was evacuated and that Lee had surrendered. The bells rang merrily all over the land. The booming of cannon was heard, illuminations and torchlight processions manifested the general joy, and families were looking for the speedy return of their loved ones from the field of battle. Just in the wildest joy, in one hour, nay, in one moment the tidings thrilled throughout the land that Abraham Lincoln, the best of Presidents, had perished by the hands of an assassin, and then all that feeling which had been gathering for four years in the form of excitement, grief, horror, and joy, turned into one wail of woe; a sadness inexpressible, an anguish unutterable; but it was not the times, merely, which caused the mourning. The mode of his death must be taken into the account. Had he died on a bed of sickness, with kind friends around him; had the sweat of death been wiped from his brow by gentle hands while he was yet conscious; could he have had power to speak words of affection to his stricken widow; words of comfort to us, like those which we heard in parting, and at Washington, in his inaugural, which shall now be immortal; but it would have softened or assuaged something of the grief—there might at least have been preparation for the event. But no moment of warning was given to him or to us. He was stricken down, too, when his hopes for the end of the rebellion were bright, and the prospect of a joyous life was before him.

There was a Cabinet meeting that day, said to have been

the most cheerful and happy of any held since the beginning of the rebellion. After this meeting he talked with his friends, and spoke of the four years of tempest; of the storm being over; and of the four years of pleasure and joy now awaiting him, as the weight of care or anguish would be taken from his mind, and he could have happy days with his family again. In the midst of his anticipations, he left his house never to return alive. The evening was Good Friday—the saddest day in the whole calendar for the Christian church, henceforth, in this country to be made sadder, if possible, by the memory of the nation's loss; and so filled with grief was every Christian heart, that even all the joyous thought of Easter Sunday failed to move the crushing sorrow, under which the true worshipper bowed in the house of God.

But the great cause of this mourning is to be found in the man himself. Mr. Lincoln was no ordinary man, and I believe the conviction has been growing on the nation's mind, as it certainly has been on my own, especially in the last years of his administration, that, by the hand of God, he was especially singled out to guide our Government in these troublous times, and, it seems to me, that the hand of God may be traced in many of the events connected with his history.

First, then, I recognize this in the physical education which he received, and which prepared him for enduring herculean labor, in the toils of his boyhood and the labors of his manhood, God was giving him an iron frame. Next to this was his identification with the heart of the great people, understanding their feelings, because he was one of them, and connected with them in their movements and life. His education was simple: a few months spent in a school-house, which gave him the elements of education. He read a few books, but mastered all he read. Bunyan's Pilgrim's Progress, fables, and the Life of Washington, were his favorites. In these we recognize the works which gave the bias to his character, and which partly molded his style. His early life, with its varied struggles, joined him indissolubly to the working masses, and no elevation in society diminished his respect for the sons of toil. He knew what it was to fell the tall trees of the forest, and to stem the current of the hard Mississippi. His home was in the growing West, the heart of the Republic, and, invigorated by the wind which swept over its prairies, he learned lessons of self-reliance, which sustained him in seasons of adversity. His genius was soon recognized, as true genius always will be, and he was placed in the Legislature of his State. Already acquainted with the principles of law, he devoted his thoughts to matters of public interest, and soon began to be looked upon as the coming statesman.

As early as 1849 he presented resolutions in the Legislature, asking for emancipation in the District of Columbia, while, with but rare exceptions, the whole popular mind of his State was opposed to the measure. From that hour he was a steady and uniform friend of humanity, and was preparing for the conflict of later years.

You ask me on what mental characteristics his greatness rested. I answer, on a quick and ready perception of facts; on a memory unusually tenacious and retentive; and on a logical turn of mind, which followed sternly and unwaveringly every link in the chain of thought, on any subject which he was called on to investigate. I think there have been minds more broad in their character, more comprehensive in their scope; but I doubt if ever there has been a man who could follow step by step, with logical power, the points which he desired to illustrate. He gained this power by a close study of geometry, and by a determination to persevere in the truth in its relations and simplicity.

It is said of him that in childhood, when he had any difficulty in listening to a conversation to ascertain what people meant, if he tried to rest, he could not sleep until he tried to understand the precise points intended, and when understood, to convey them in a clearer manner to those who did not. Who that has read his messages fails to perceive the directness and the simplicity of his style; and this very trait, which was scoffed at and derided by opponents, is now recognized as one of the strong points of that mighty mind which has so powerfully influenced the destiny of this nation, and which shall for ages to come influence the destiny of humanity.

It is not, however, chiefly by his mental faculties that he gained such control over mankind. His moral power gave him pre-eminence. The convictions of men that Abraham Lincoln was an honest man, led them to yield to his guidance. As has been said of Mr. Cobden, whom he greatly respected, he made every man feel a better sense of himself—a recognizement of individuality—a self-relying power. They saw in him a man whom they believed would do what was right, regardless of all consequences. It was the moral feeling which gave him the greatest hold on the people, and made his utterances almost oracular.

When the nation was angered by the perfidy of foreign nations in allowing privateers to be fitted out, he uttered the significant expression, "One war at a time," and it stilled the national heart. When his own friends were divided as to what steps should be taken as to slavery, that simple utterance, "I will save the Union, if I can, with slavery; but if not slavery must perish; for the Union must be preserved"—became the rallying word. Men felt the struggle was for the Union, and all other questions must be subsidiary. But after all, by the acts of a man shall his fame be perpetuated. Much praise is due to the men who aided him. He called able counselors around him, and able Generals into the field—men who have borne the sword as bravely as ever any human arm has borne it. He had the aid of prayerful and thoughtful men every-where, but under his own guiding hands the movements of our land have been conducted. Turn toward the different departments. We had an unorganized militia, a mere skeleton army, yet, under his care, that army has been enlarged into a force, which, for skill, intelligence, efficiency and bravery, surpasses any which the world has ever seen. Before its veterans, the face of even the renowned veterans of Napoleon shall pale. [Applause.] And the mothers and sisters on these hill-sides, and all over the land, shall take to their arms again braver men than ever fought in European wars. The reason is obvious. Money, or a desire for fame collected those armies, or they were rallied to sustain favorite thrones or dynasties; but the armies he called into being fought for liberty, for the Union, and for the right of self-government; and many of them felt that the battles they won were for humanity every-where and for all time; for I believe that God has not suffered this terrible rebellion to come upon our land merely for a chastisement to us, or a lesson to our age. There are moments which involve in themselves eternities. There are instants which seem to contain germs which shall develop and bloom forever. Such a moment came in the tide of time, to our land, when a question must be settled—the power of affecting all the earth. The contest was for human freedom, not for this Republic merely; not for the Union simply, but to decide whether the people, as a people, in their entire majesty, were destined to be the Government, or whether they were to be subject to tyrants or autocrats, or to class rule of any kind.

This is the great question for which we have been fighting, and its decision is at hand; and the result of the contest will affect the ages to come. If successful, republics will spread, in spite of monarchs, all over this earth. [Exclamations of "Amen;" "Thank God."]

I turn from the army to the navy. What was it when the war commenced? Now we have our ships of war at home and abroad to guard privateers in foreign sympathizing ports, as well as to care for every part of our own coast. They have taken forts that military men said could not be taken; and a brave Admiral, for the first time in the world's history, lashes himself to the mast, there to remain as long as he had a particle of skill or strength to watch over his ship while it engaged in the perilous contest of taking the strong forts of the enemy.

Then, again, I turn to the Treasury Department. Where should the money come from? Wise men predicted ruin; but our national credit has been maintained and our currency is safer to-day than it ever was before. Not only so, but through our national bonds, if properly used, we shall have a permanent basis for currency, and an investment so desirable for capitalists of other nations, that under the laws of trade, I believe the center of exchange will be transferred from England to the United States.

But the great act of the mighty chieftain, on which his fame shall rest long after his frame shall molder away, is that of giving freedom to a race. We have all been taught to revere the sacred characters. We have thought of Moses, of his power, and the prominence he gave to the moral law, and how his name now towers high among the names in heaven, and how he delivered three millions of his kindred out of bondage; and yet we may assert that Abraham Lincoln, by his proclamation, liberated more enslaved people than ever Moses set free, and those not of his kindred or of his race. Such a power or such an opportunity has seldom been given to man. When other events shall have been forgotten; when the world shall become a net-work of republics; when every throne shall have been swept from the face of the earth; when literature shall enlighten all minds; when the claims of humanity shall be recognized everywhere, this act shall still be conspicuous on the pages of history; and we are thankful that God gave to Abraham Lincoln the decision and wisdom and grace to issue that proclamation, which stands high above all other papers which have been penned by uninspired men. [Applause.]

Abraham Lincoln was a good man; he was known as an honest, temperate, forgiving man; a just man; a man of a noble heart in every way. As to his religious experience, I cannot speak definately, because I was not privi'eged to know much of his private sentiments. My acquaintance with him did not give me the opportunity to hear him speak on those topics. This I know, however, he read the Bible frequently, loved it for its great truths, and profound teachings; and he tried to be guided by its precepts. He believed in Christ, the Saviour of sinners, and I think he was sincerely trying to bring his life into the principles of revealed religion. Certainly, if there ever was a man who illustrated some of the principles of pure religion, that man was our departed President. Look over all his speeches; listen to his utterances. He never spoke unkindly of any man; even the rebels received no words of anger from him; and the last day illustrated, in a remarkable manner, his forgiving disposition. A dispatch was received that afternoon, that Thompson and Tucker were trying to make their escape through Maine, and it was proposed to arrest them. Mr. Lincoln, however, preferred, rather to let them quietly escape. He was seeking to save the very men who had been plotting his destruction, and this morning we read a proclamation offering $25,000 for the arrest of these men, as aiders and abettors of assassination. So that in his expiring acts he was saying, " Father, forgive them; they know not what they do."

To the address of a large religious body he replied; " Thanks be unto God, who, in our national trials, giveth us the churches." To a minister who said "he hoped the Lord was on our side," he replied that it gave him no concern whether the Lord was on our side or not, "for" he added " I know the Lord is always on the side of right"; and with deep feeling added, " but God is my witness that it is my constant anxiety and prayer that both myself and this nation should be on the Lord's side."

As a rule, I doubt if any President has ever shown such a trust in God, or in public documents so frequently referred to Divine aid. Often did he remark to friends and to delegations that his hope for our success rested in his conviction that God would bless our efforts, because we were trying to do right.

In his domestic life he was exceedingly kind and affectionate. He was a devoted husband and father. During his Presidential term he lost his second son, Willie. To an officer of the army he said not long since: "Do you ever find yourself talking with the dead?" and added—"Since Willie's death, I catch myself every day involuntarily talking with him as if he were with me."

On his widow, who is unable to be here, I need only invoke the blessing of Almighty God, that she may be comforted and sustained. For his son, who has witnessed the exercises of this hour, all that I can desire is that the mantle of his father may fall upon him. [Exclamations of "Amen."]

Let us pause a moment on the lesson of the hour before we part. This man, though he fell by an assassin, still fell under the permissive hand of God. He had some wise purpose in allowing him so to fall. What more could he have desired of life to himself? Were not his honors full? There was no office to which he could aspire. The popular heart clung around him as around no other man. The nations of the world had learned to honor our Chief Magistrate. If rumors of a desired alliance with

England be true, Napoleon trembled when he heard of the fall of Richmond, and asked what nation would join him to protect him against our Government.

Besides, the guidance of such a man, his fame, was full; his work was done, and he sealed his glory by becoming the nation's great martyr for liberty.

He appears to have had a strange presentiment early in his political life that some day he would be President. You see it indicated in 1839. Of the slave power he said: "Broken by it I too may be; bow to it I never will. The probability that we may fail in this struggle, ought not to deter us from the support of a cause which we deem to be just. It shall not deter me. If ever I feel the soul within me elevate and expand to those dimensions not wholly unworthy of its Almighty architect, it is when I contemplate the cause of my country. Deserted by all the world beside, and standing up boldly and alone, and hurling defiance at her victorious oppressors; here, without contemplating consequences, before high heaved and in the face of the world, I swear eternal fidelity to the just cause, as I deem it, of the land of my life, my liberty, and my love." And yet secretly he said to more than one, "I never shall live out the four years of my term. When the rebellion is crushed, my work is done." So it was. He lived to see the last battle fought, and to dictate a dispatch from the home of Jefferson Davis; lived till the power of the rebellion was broken, and then, having done the work for which God had sent him, angels, I trust, were sent to shield him from one moment of pain or suffering, and to bear him from this world to that high and glorious realm where the patriot and the good shall live forever.

His example teaches young men that every position of eminence is open before the diligent and the worthy, to the active men of the country. His example urges the country to trust in God and do right.

Standing as we do to-day, by his coffin and sepulcher, let us resolve to carry forward the policy which he so nobly began. Let us do right to all men. Let us vow, in the sight of Heaven, eradicate every vestige of human slavery; to give every human being his true position before God and man; to crush every form of rebellion, and to stand by the flag which God has given us. How joyful that it floated over a part of every State before Mr. Lincoln's career was ended.

How singular that, to the fact of the assassin's heel being caught in the folds of the flag, we are probably indebted for his capture. The flag and the traitor must ever be enemies.

Traitors will probably suffer by the change of rulers, for one of sterner mold, and who himself has deeply suffered from the rebellion, now wields the sword of justice.

Our country, too, is stronger for the trial. A republic was declared by monarchists to weak to endure a civil war. Yet we have crushed the most gigantic rebellion in history, and have grown in strength and population every year of the struggle. We have passed through the ordeal of a popular election, while swords and bayonets were in the field, and have come out unharmed.

And now in an hour of excitement, with a large minority having preferred another man for President, the bullet of the assassin has laid our President prostrate. Has there been a mutiny? Has any rival proposed his claims? Out of an army of near a million, no officer or soldier uttered one note of dissent; and in an hour or two after Mr. Lincoln's death, another leader, with constitutional powers, occupied his chair, and the Government moved forward without a single jar. The world will learn that republics are the strongest governments on earth.

To the ambitious there is this fearful lesson: Of the four candidates for Presidential honors in 1860, two of them, Douglas and Lincoln, once competitors—but now sleeping patriots—rest from their labors; Bell perished in poverty and misery, as a traitor might perish, and Breckinridge is a frightened fugitive, with the brand of traitor on his brow.

And now, my friends, in the words of the departed, "With malice toward none;" free from all feeling of personal vengeance, yet believing the sword must not be borne in vain, let us go forward, even in painful duty. Let every man who was a Senator, or Representative in Congress, and who aided in beginning this rebellion, and thus led to the slaughter of our sons and daughters, be brought to speedy and to certain punishment. Let every officer educated at public expense, and who, having been advanced to position has perjured himself, and has turned his sword against the vitals of his country, be doomed to a felon's death. This, I believe, is the will of the American people. Men may attempt to compromise and to restore these traitors and murderers to society again, but the American people will rise in their majesty and sweep all such compromises and compromisers away, and shall declare that there shall be no peace to rebels.

But to the deluded masses we shall extend arms of forgiveness. We will take them to our hearts. We will walk with them side by side, as we go forward to work out a glorious destiny. The time will come when, in the beautiful words of him whose lips are now forever sealed, "the mystic cords of memory, which stretch from every battle-field and from every patriot's grave shall yield a sweeter music when touched by the angels of our better nature."

The closing prayer was offered up by Dr. Harkey. Next in continuation was the requiem, "Peace, troubled soul," the benediction by Dr. P. D. Gurley, the President's former pastor, and last of all, a funeral hymn, composed by Dr. Gurley for the occasion, and the doxology:

> Rest, noble martyr! rest in peace;
> Rest with the true and brave,
> Who, like thee, fell in Freedom's cause,
> The Nation's life to save.
>
> Thy name shall live while time endures,
> And men shall say of thee,
> "He saved his country from its foes,
> And bade the slave be free."
>
> These deeds shall be thy monument,
> Better than brass or stone;
> They leave thy fame in glory's light,
> Unrival'd and alone.
>
> This consecrated spot shall be
> To Freedom ever dear;
> And Freedom's sons of every race
> Shall weep and worship here.
>
> O God! before whom we, in tears,
> Our fallen Chief deplore,
> Grant that the cause, for which he died,
> May live for evermore.

DOXOLOGY.

> To Father, Son, and Holy Ghost,
> The God whom we adore,
> Be glory as it was, is now,
> And shall be evermore.

REMINISCENCES AND INCIDENTS.

MR. LINCOLN AND JOHN E. McDONOUGH, THE ACTOR.

In an address delivered on the 24th of April by Hon. W. D. Kelly before the Girls' High and Normal School of Philadelphia, the speaker referred to a number of interesting incidents in the life and character of Mr. Lincoln, and among other things spoke of an interview between Mr. Lincoln and the well-known actor, John E. McDonough. Mr. Kelly thus describes this meeting:

On a very rainy night during the session of Congress preceding the last, I found at my room Rev. Benjamin R. Miller, Chaplain of the 118th Pennsylvania Volunteers, and Mr. John E. McDonough, the actor, who was on the next night to begin playing in Washington his extravaganza of the "Seven Sisters," by which he had done considerable in promoting patriotic feeling among the young people in the country. Duty and pleasure prompted me to give the evening to them in some way, and I felt that I might do good to them, perhaps to myself—perhaps to my country, too—by taking them to see our good President. I proposed that we should go; they readily assented, and we started at once for the White House. We found Mr. Lincoln alone; and, on entering, I said to him that we had come to trouble him professionally, and probably to perplex him somewhat, as we represented three professions—the law, divinity and the histrionic profession. I introduced my friend Miller as the reverend chaplain, and Mr. McDonough as "Mrs. Pluto," the name of the character he sustained in the extravaganza.

"Well," said the President, "pray tell me, how do your chaplain and 'Mrs. Pluto' get along together? I should think there might be some discord in a family made up of such materials."

They were soon seated, at his bidding, and, after a few words to the chaplain, who had come from the field, he turned to Mr. McDonough and said:—

"I am very glad to see you, sir, for I want to learn something of Shakespeare. I don't get much time to study his writings, and I want to put some questions to you that I put to Mr. Hackett. I will tell you, frankly, that Mr. Hackett's replies, on one or two of the points, were very unsatisfactory to me; they almost impressed me with a doubt as to whether he studies Shakespeare thoroughly, or only the acting plays."

Raising from his seat, he went to a shelf, and took down his volumes of Shakespeare. Having found the passage, in "Henry "IV." about which he desired to inquire, he read a portion of it, and said to Mr. McDonough, "Can you tell me why that is omitted from the acting play? There is nothing in all Shakespeare—certainly nothing in 'Henry IV.' or the 'Merry Wives of Windsor'—that equals it in wit and humor." Mr. McDonough gave him what he believed to be his reasons—those which were conclusive with him.

The President said:—"Those are more satisfactory than Mr. Hackett's reasons, but they do not entirely satisfy me." Then turning to my friend Mr. Miller, he said:—"Probably you do not know that the acting plays are not the plays as Shakespeare wrote them. 'Richard III.,' for instance, begins with passages from 'Henry VI.;' then you get a portion of 'Richard III.;' then more of 'Henry VI.;' and then there is one of the best known soliloques, which is not Shakespeare's at all, but was written by quite another man—by Colley Cibber—was it not, Mr. McDonough?"

Branching off from Shakespeare, Mr. Lincoln cited brief passages from Byron, Rogers, Campbell, Moore, and I think a short one from Shelley, always running a parallel between the passage he quoted and some passage or scene in Shakespeare. Finally he said:—"But there is a great deal of very fine poetry floating about anonymously. There is one poem that is almost continually present with me; it crosses my mind whenever I have relief from thought and care." He then recited some verses of the poem, which Mr. Carpenter was fortunate enough to indite from his lips:—

OH, WHY SHOULD THE SPIRIT OF MORTAL BE PROUD.
Oh, why should the spirit of mortal be proud?
Like a swift, fleeting meteor, a fast flying cloud,
A flash of the lightning, a break of the wave,
He passeth from life to his rest in the grave.

The leaves of the oak and the willow shall fade,
Be scattered around and together be laid;
And the young and the old, and the low and the high,
Shall moulder to dust and together shall lie.

The infant a mother attended and loved,
The mother that infant's affection who proved;
The husband that mother and infant who blessed,
Each, all, are away to their dwellings of rest.

The hand of the king that the sceptre hath borne;
The brow of the priest that the mitre hath worn;
The eye of the sage and the heart of the brave,
Are hidden and lost in the depth of the grave.

The peasant, whose lot was to sow and to reap;
The herdsman who climbed with his goats up the steep;
The beggar, who wandered in search of his bread,
Have faded away like the grass that we tread.

So the multitude goes, like the flower or the weed,
That withers away to let others succeed;
So the multitude comes, even those we behold,
To repeat every tale that has often been told.

For we are the same that our fathers have been;
We see the same sights that our father's have seen,
We drink the same stream and view the same sun,
And run the same course our fathers have run.

The thoughts we are thinking our fathers would think;
From the death we are shrinking our fathers would shrink;
To the life we are clinging they also will cling;
But it speeds for us all, like a bird on the wing.

They loved, but the story we cannot unfold;
They scorned, but the heart of the haughty is cold;
They grieved, but no wail from their slumber will come;
They joyed, but the tongue of their gladness is dumb.

They died, ay! they died; we things that are now,
That walk on the turf that lies over their brow,
And make in their dwellings a transient abode,
Meet the things that they met on their pilgrimage road.

Yea! hope and despondency, pleasure and pain,
We mingle together in sunshine and rain;
And the smile and the tear, the song and the dirge,
Still follow each other, like surge upon surge.

'Tis the wink of an eye, 'tis the draft of a breath;
From the blossom of health to the paleness of death,
From the gilded saloon to the bier and the shroud,
Oh, why should the spirit of mortal be proud?

"Now," said he, "I do not know where there is anything truer, more touching, more rhythmical than that: and I wish that if any of you should chance at any time to learn the name of the author, you would let me know it. I have known the poem for years, but I have never been able to learn who wrote it, and I want to regard him by name as a friend." Do you mark why he wanted to know the author? He wanted to know the name that he might love the individual who had given him so much pleasure. When we parted from him, he said:

"Gentlemen, I am deeply grateful to you for this visit. The heavy rain that has kept other visitors away has been a comfort to me. Since I became a candidate for the Presidency, I have not enjoyed two consecutive hours of conversation on literature until to-night, and I feel so refreshed that if I could only hope to have the time; I would beg you to come soon again."

MR. COLFAX ON MR. LINCOLN.

In the memorial addresses, delivered in Chicago, on the character of Abraham Lincoln, Mr. Colfax, of Indiana, related of the late President the following:

One morning, over two years ago, calling upon him on business, I found him looking more than usually pale and careworn, and inquired the reason. He replied that the bad news he had received at a late hour the previous night, which had not yet been communicated to the press, adding that he had not closed his eyes or breakfasted; and; with an expression I never shall forget, he exclaimed; "How willingly would I exchange places to-day, with the soldier who sleeps on the ground in the Army of the Potomac."

No one could ever convince the President that he was in danger of violent death. Judging others by himself, he could not realize that any one could seek his blood. Or he may have believed as Napoleon wrote to Jerome, that no public man could effectually shield himself from the danger of assassination. Easier of access to the public at large than had been any of his predecessors, admitting his bitterest enemies to his reception rooms, alone; restive under the cavalry escort which Secretary Stanton insisted should accompany him last summer, in his daily journeys between the White House and his summer residence, at the Soldier's Home, several miles from Washington, at a time, too, as since ascertained in the details of this long organized plot, discovered since his death, when it was intended to gag and hand-cuff him, and to carry him to the rebel capitol as a hostage for their recognition; sometimes escaping from their escort, by anticipating their usual hour of attendance; walking about the gardens unattended; he could not be persuaded that he ran any risk whatever. Being at City Point after the evacuation of Richmond, he determined to go thither, not from idle curiosity, but to see if he could not do something to stop the effusion of blood, and hasten the peace for which he longed.

The ever watchful Secretary of War hearing of it, implored him, by telegraph, not to go, and warned him that some lurking assassin might take his life. But, armed with his good intentions—alas, how feeble a shield they proved against the death-blow afterward—he went, walked fearlessly and carelessly through the streets—met and conferred with a rebel leader, who had remained there; and when he returned to City Point, telegraphed to his faithful friend and constitutional adviser, who till then had feared, as we all did at that time, for his life, "I received your dispatch last night, went to Richmond this morning, and have just returned—Abraham Lincoln." When I told him, on that last night, how uneasy all had been at his going, he replied, pleasantly and with a smile, (I quote his exact words): "Why if any one else had been President and gone to Richmond, I would have been alarmed too; but I was not scared about myself a bit." If any of you have ever been at Washington, you will remember the foot-path lined and embowered with trees leading from the back door of the War Department to the White House. One night and but recently, too, when in his anxiety for news from the army, he had been with the Secretary in the telegraph office of the department, he was starting home at a late hour by this short route. Mr. Stanton stopped him and said, "You ought not to go that way; it is dangerous for you even in the daytime, but worse at night." Mr. Lincoln replied, "I don't believe there's *any* danger there, day or night." Mr. Stanton replied solemnly, "Well, Mr. President, you shall not be killed returning that way from my department while I am in it; you *must* let me take you round by the avenue in my carriage." And Mr. Lincoln joining the Secretary on his imperious military orders and his needless alarm on his account, as he called it, entered the carriage and was driven by the well-lighted avenue to the White House.

ABRAHAM LINCOLN—AN ODE.

A noble poem, by R. H. Stoddard, entitled "Abraham Lincoln, an Oration Ode," has just been published in New York. The following stanzas describe the funeral procession through the States, and are worthy the great occasion:

Peace! Let the long procession come
For hark!—the mournful muffled drum—
    The trumpet's wail afar—
    And see! the awful Car!

Peace! Let the sad procession go,
While cannon boom, and bells toll slow;
    And go, thou sacred Car,
    Bearing our Woe afar!

Go, darkly borne, from State to State,
Whose, loyal, sorrowing cities wait
    To honor all they can
    The dust of that Good Man!

Go, grandly borne, with such a train
As greatest kings might die to gain;
    The Just, the Wise, the Brave
    Attend thee to the grave!

And you, the soldiers of our wars,
Bronzed veterans, grim with noble scars,
    Salute him once again,
    Your late Commander—slain!

Yes, let your tears, indignant, fall,
But leave your muskets on the wall;
    Your Country needs you now
    Beside the forge, the plow!

(When Justice shall unsheath her brand—
If Mercy may not stay her hand,
    Nor would we have it so—
    She must direct the blow)!

*   *   *   *   *   *.

So sweetly, sadly, sternly goes
The Fallen to his last repose;
  Beneath no mighty dome
  But in his modest Home!

The church-yard where his children rest,
The quiet spot that suits him best;
  There shall his grave be made,
  And there his bones be laid!

And there his countrymen shall come,
With memory proud, with pity dumb,
  And strangers far and near,
  For many and many a year!

For many a year, and many an age,
While History on her ample page,
  The virtues shall enroll
  Of that Paternal Soul.

www.ingramcontent.com/pod-product-compliance
Lightning Source LLC
Chambersburg PA
CBHW031455160426
43195CB00010BB/991